The Honest Whore by Thomas Dekker

IN TWO PARTS. PART THE SECOND.

Thomas Dekker was a playwright, pamphleteer and poet who, perhaps, deserves greater recognition than he has so far gained.

Despite the fact only perhaps twenty of his plays were published, and fewer still survive, he was far more prolific than that. Born around 1572 his peak years were the mid 1590's to the 1620's – seven of which he spent in a debtor's prison. His works span the late Elizabethan and Caroline eras and his numerous collaborations with Ford, Middleton, Webster and Jonson say much about his work.

His pamphlets detail much of the life in these times, times of great change, of plague and of course that great capital city London a swirling mass of people, power, intrigue.

Index of Contents
DRAMATIS PERSONÆ
SCENE—MILAN
ACT THE FIRST
SCENE I.—A Hall in Hippolito's House
SCENE II.—An Apartment in the Duke's Palace
ACT THE SECOND
SCENE I.—A Room in Matheo's House
SCENE II.—Before Candido's Shop
ACT THE THIRD
SCENE I.—An Apartment in Hippolito's House
SCENE II.—A Room in Matheo's House
SCENE III.—Before Candido's Shop
ACT THE FOURTH
SCENE I.—A Room in Matheo's House
SCENE II.—An Apartment in the Duke's Palace
SCENE III.—A Room in Matheo's House
ACT THE FIFTH
SCENE I.—A Street
SCENE II.—An Apartment in Bridewell
Thomas Dekker – A Short Biography
Thomas Dekker – A Concise Bibliography

DRAMATIS PERSONÆ.
GASPARO TREBAZZI, Duke of Milan.
HIPPOLITO, a Count, Husband of INFELICE.
ORLANDO , Father of BELLAFRONT.
MATHEO, Husband of BELLAFRONT.

CANDIDO, a Linen Draper.
LODOVICO SFORZA.
BERALDO.
CAROLO.
FONTINELL.
ASTOLFO.
ANTONIO GEORGIO, a poor Scholar.
BRYAN, an Irish Footman.
BOTS, a Pander.
Masters of Bridewell, Prentices, Servants, &c.

INFELICE, Wife of HIPPOLITO.
BELLAFRONT, Wife of MATHEO.
CANDIDO'S Bride.
Mistress HORSELEECH, a Bawd.
DOROTHEA TARGET,   }
PENELOPE WHOREHOUND, } Harlots.
CATHARINA BOUNTINALL, }

SCENE—MILAN.

ACT THE FIRST.

SCENE I.—A Hall in Hippolito's House.

On one side enter BERALDO, CAROLO, FONTINELL, and ASTOLFO, with SERVING MEN, or PAGES, attending on them; on the other side enter LODOVICO.

LODOVICO
Good day, gallants.

ALL
Good morrow, sweet Lodovico.

LODOVICO
How dost thou, Carolo?

CAROLO
Faith, as the physicians do in a plague, see the world sick, and am well myself.

FONTINELL
Here's a sweet morning, gentlemen.

LODOVICO

Oh, a morning to tempt Jove from his ningle,[1] Ganymede; which is but to give dairy-wenches green gowns as they are going a-milking. What, is thy lord stirring yet?

[1] Favourite.

ASTOLFO
Yes, he will not be horsed this hour, sure.

BERALDO
My lady swears he shall, for she longs to be at court.

CAROLO
Oh, we shall ride switch and spur; would we were there once.

Enter BRYAN.

LODOVICO
How now, is thy lord ready?

BRYAN
No, so crees sa' me, my lady will have some little ting in her pelly first.

CAROLO
Oh, then they'll to breakfast.

LODOVICO
Footman, does my lord ride i'th' coach with my lady, or on horseback?

BRYAN
No, foot, la, my lady will have me lord sheet wid her, my lord will sheet in de one side, and my lady sheet in de toder side.

[Exit.

LODOVICO
My lady sheet in de toder side! Did you ever hear a rascal talk so like a pagan? Is't not strange that a fellow of his star, should be seen here so long in Italy, yet speak so from a Christian?

Enter ANTONIO, with a book.

ASTOLFO
An Irishman in Italy! that so strange! why, the nation have running heads. [They walk up and down.

LODOVICO
Nay, Carolo, this is more strange, I ha' been in France, there's few of them. Marry, England they count a warm chimney corner, and there they swarm like crickets to the crevice of a brew-house; but sir, in England I have noted one thing.

ASTOLFO, BERALDO, &c.
What's that, what's that of England?

LODOVICO
Marry this, sir,—what's he yonder?

BERALDO
A poor fellow would speak with my lord.

LODOVICO
In England, sir,—troth, I ever laugh when I think on't: to see a whole nation should be marked i'th' forehead, as a man may say, with one iron: why, sir, there all costermongers are Irishmen.

CAROLO
Oh, that's to show their antiquity, as coming from Eve, who was an apple-wife, and they take after the mother.

ASTOLFO, BERALDO, &c.
Good, good! ha, ha!

LODOVICO
Why, then, should all your chimney-sweepers likewise be Irishmen? answer that now; come, your wit.

CAROLO
Faith, that's soon answered, for St. Patrick, you know, keeps purgatory; he makes the fire, and his countrymen could do nothing, if they cannot sweep the chimneys.

ASTOLFO, BERALDO, &c.
Good again.

LODOVICO
Then, sir, have you many of them, like this fellow, especially those of his hair, footmen to noblemen and others,[2] and the knaves are very faithful where they love. By my faith, very proper men many of them, and as active as the clouds,—whirr, hah!

[2] *The running footmen of those days were generally Irishmen.*

ASTOLFO, BERALDO, &c.
Are they so?

LODOVICO
And stout! exceeding stout; why, I warrant, this precious wild villain, if he were put to't, would fight more desperately than sixteen Dunkirks.[3]

[3] *Meaning Dunkirk privateers.*

ASTOLFO
The women, they say, are very fair.

LODOVICO
No, no, our country buona-robas,[4] oh! are the sugarest, delicious rogues!

[4] *Buona roba is an Italian phrase for a courtesan.*

ASTOLFO
Oh, look, he has a feeling of them!

LODOVICO
Not I, I protest. There's a saying when they commend nations. It goes, the Irishman for his hand, the Welshman for a leg, the Englishman for a face, the Dutchman for a beard.

FONTINELL
I'faith, they may make swabbers of them.

LODOVICO
The Spaniard,—let me see,—for a little foot, I take it; the Frenchman,—what a pox hath he? and so of the rest. Are they at breakfast yet? come walk.

ASTOLFO
This Lodovico is a notable tongued fellow.

FONTINELL
Discourses well.

BERALDO
And a very honest gentleman.

ASTOLFO
Oh! he's well valued by my lord.

Enter BELLAFRONT, with a petition.

FONTINELL
How now, how now, what's she?

BERALDO
Let's make towards her.

BELLAFRONT
Will it be long, sir, ere my lord come forth?

ASTOLFO
Would you speak with my lord?

LODOVICO
How now, what's this, a nurse's bill? hath any here got thee with child and now will not keep it?

BELLAFRONT
No, sir, my business is unto my lord.

LODOVICO
He's about his own wife's now, he'll hardly dispatch two causes in a morning.

ASTOLFO
No matter what he says, fair lady; he's a knight, there's no hold to be taken at his words.

FONTINELL
My lord will pass this way presently.

BERALDO
A pretty, plump rogue.

ASTOLFO
A good lusty, bouncing baggage.

BERALDO
Do you know her?

LODOVICO
A pox on her, I was sure her name was in my table-book once; I know not of what cut her die is now, but she has been more common than tobacco: this is she that had the name of the Honest Whore.

ASTOLFO, BERALDO &c.
Is this she?

LODOVICO
This is the blackamoor that by washing was turned white: this is the birding-piece new scoured: this is she that, if any of her religion can be saved, was saved by my lord Hippolito.

ASTOLFO
She has been a goodly creature.

LODOVICO
She has been! that's the epitaph of all whores. I'm well acquainted with the poor gentleman her husband. Lord! what fortunes that man has overreached! She knows not me, yet I have been in her company; I scarce know her, for the beauty of her cheek hath, like the moon, suffered strange eclipses since I beheld it: but women are like medlars,—no sooner ripe but rotten:

A woman last was made, but is spent first.
Yet man is oft proved in performance worst.

ASTOLFO, BERALDO &c.
My lord is come.

Enter HIPPOLITO, INFELICE, and two WAITING WOMEN.

HIPPOLITO
We ha' wasted half this morning. Morrow, Lodovico.

LODOVICO
Morrow, madam.

HIPPOLITO
Let's away to horse.

LODOVICO, ASTOLFO, &c
Ay, ay, to horse, to horse.

BELLAFRONT
I do beseech your lordship, let your eye read o'er this wretched paper.

HIPPOLITO
I'm in haste, pray thee, good woman, take some apter time.

INFELICE
Good woman, do.

BELLAFRONT
Oh 'las! it does concern a poor man's life.

HIPPOLITO
Life! sweetheart?—Seat yourself, I'll but read this and come.

LODOVICO
What stockings have you put on this morning, madam? If they be not yellow,[5] change them; that paper is a letter from some wench to your husband.

[5] Yellow was typical of jealousy.

INFELICE
Oh sir, that cannot make me jealous.

[Exeunt all except HIPPOLITO, BELLAFRONT, and ANTONIO.

HIPPOLITO
Your business, sir? to me?

ANTONIO
Yes, my good lord.

HIPPOLITO
Presently, sir.—Are you Matheo's wife?

BELLAFRONT
That most unfortunate woman.

HIPPOLITO
I'm sorry these storms are fallen on him; I love Matheo,
And any good shall do him; he and I
Have sealed two bonds of friendship, which are strong
In me, however fortune does him wrong.
He speaks here he's condemned. Is't so?

BELLAFRONT
Too true.

HIPPOLITO
What was he whom he killed? Oh, his name's here;
Old Giacomo, son to the Florentine;
Giacomo, a dog, that to meet profit,
Would to the very eyelids wade in blood
Of his own children. Tell Matheo,
The duke, my father, hardly shall deny
His signèd pardon; 'twas fair fight, yes,
If rumour's tongue go true; so writes he here.—
To-morrow morning I return from court,
Pray be you here then.—I'll have done, sir, straight:— [To ANTONIO.
But in troth say, are you Matheo's wife?
You have forgot me.

BELLAFRONT
No, my lord.

HIPPOLITO
Your turner,
That made you smooth to run an even bias,
You know I loved you when your very soul
Was full of discord: art not a good wench still?

BELLAFRONT
Umph, when I had lost my way to Heaven, you showed it:
I was new born that day.

Re-enter LODOVICO.

LODOVICO
'Sfoot, my lord, your lady asks if you have not left your wench yet? When you get in once, you never have done. Come, come, come, pay your old score, and send her packing; come.

HIPPOLITO

Ride softly on before, I'll o'ertake you.

LODOVICO
Your lady swears she'll have no riding on before, without ye.

HIPPOLITO
Prithee, good Lodovico.

Lod. My lord, pray hasten.

HIPPOLITO
I come.

[Exit LODOVICO.

To-morrow let me see you, fare you well;
Commend me to Matheo. Pray one word more:
Does not your father live about the court?

BELLAFRONT
I think he does, but such rude spots of shame
Stick on my cheek, that he scarce knows my name.

HIPPOLITO
Orlando, is't not?

BELLAFRONT
Yes, my lord.

HIPPOLITO
What does he for you?

BELLAFRONT
All he should: when children
From duty start, parents from love may swerve;
He nothing does: for nothing I deserve.

HIPPOLITO
Shall I join him unto you, and restore you to wonted grace?

BELLAFRONT
It is impossible.

HIPPOLITO
It shall be put to trial: fare you well.

[Exit BELLAFRONT.

The face I would not look on! Sure then 'twas rare,
When in despite of grief, 'tis still thus fair.
Now, sir, your business with me.

ANTONIO
I am bold
T'express my love and duty to your lordship
In these few leaves.

HIPPOLITO
A book!

ANTONIO
Yes, my good lord.

HIPPOLITO
Are you a scholar?

ANTONIO
Yes, my lord, a poor one.

HIPPOLITO
Sir, you honour me.
Kings may be scholars' patrons, but, faith, tell me,
To how many hands besides hath this bird flown,
How many partners share with me?

ANTONIO
Not one,
In troth, not one: your name I held more dear;
I'm not, my lord, of that low character.

HIPPOLITO
Your name I pray?

ANTONIO
Antonio Georgio.

HIPPOLITO
Of Milan?

ANTONIO
Yes, my lord.

HIPPOLITO
I'll borrow leave
To read you o'er, and then we'll talk: till then
Drink up this gold; good wits should love good wine;

This of your loves, the earnest that of mine.—

[Gives money.

Re-enter BRYAN.

How now, sir, where's your lady? not gone yet?

BRYAN
I fart di lady is run away from dee, a mighty deal of ground, she sent me back for dine own sweet face, I pray dee come, my lord, away, wu't tow go now?

HIPPOLITO
Is the coach gone? Saddle my horse, the sorrel.

BRYAN
A pox a' de horse's nose, he is a lousy rascally fellow, when I came to gird his belly, his scurvy guts rumbled; di horse farted in my face, and dow knowest, an Irishman cannot abide a fart. But I have saddled de hobby-horse, di fine hobby is ready, I pray dee my good sweet lord, wi't tow go now, and I will run to de devil before dee?

HIPPOLITO
Well, sir,—I pray let's see you, master scholar.

BRYAN
Come, I pray dee, wu't come, sweet face? Go.

[Exeunt.

SCENE II.—An Apartment in the Duke's Palace.

Enter LODOVICO, CAROLO, ASTOLFO, and BERALDO.

LODOVICO
Godso', gentlemen, what do we forget?

CAROLO, ASTOLFO, BERALDO
What?

LODOVICO
Are not we all enjoined as this day.—Thursday is't not?
Ay, as this day to be at the linen-draper's house at dinner?

CAROLO
Signor Candido, the patient man.

ASTOLFO
Afore Jove, true, upon this day he's married.

BERALDO
I wonder, that being so stung with a wasp before, he dares venture again to come about the eaves amongst bees.

LODOVICO
Oh 'tis rare sucking a sweet honey comb! pray Heaven his old wife be buried deep enough, that she rise not up to call for her dance! The poor fiddlers' instruments would crack for it, she'd tickle them. At any hand let's try what mettle is in his new bride; if there be none, we'll put in some. Troth, it's a very noble citizen, I pity he should marry again; I'll walk along, for it is a good old fellow.

CAROLO
I warrant the wives of Milan would give any fellow twenty thousand ducats, that could but have the face to beg of the duke, that all the citizens in Milan might be bound to the peace of patience, as the linen-draper is.

LODOVICO
Oh, fie upon't! 'twould undo all us that are courtiers, we should have no whoop! with the wenches then.

Enter HIPPOLITO.

CAROLO, ASTOLFO, BERALDO
My lord's come.

HIPPOLITO
How now, what news?

CAROLO, ASTOLFO, BERALDO
None.

LODOVICO
Your lady is with the duke, her father.

HIPPOLITO
And we'll to them both presently—

Enter ORLANDO .

Who's that!

CAROLO, ASTOLFO, BERALDO
Signor Friscobaldo.

HIPPOLITO
Friscobaldo, oh! pray call him, and leave me, we two have business.

CAROLO
Ho Signor! Signor Friscobaldo! The Lord Hippolito.

[Exeunt all but HIPPOLITO and FRISCOBALDO.

ORLANDO
My noble lord: my Lord Hippolito! the duke's son! His brave daughter's brave husband! how does your honoured lordship! does your nobility remember so poor a gentleman as Signor Orlando Friscobaldo! Old mad Orlando!

HIPPOLITO
Oh, sir, our friends! they ought to be unto us as our jewels, as dearly valued, being locked up, and unseen, as when we wear them in our hands. I see, Friscobaldo, age hath not command of your blood, for all Time's sickle has gone over you, you are Orlando still.

ORLANDO
Why, my lord, are not the fields mown and cut down, and stripped bare, and yet wear they not pied coats again? Though my head be like a leek, white, may not my heart be like the blade, green?

HIPPOLITO
Scarce can I read the stories on your brow,
Which age hath writ there; you look youthful still.

ORLANDO
I eat snakes,[6] my lord, I eat snakes.

[6] *A supposed recipe for restoring youth.—Dyce.*

My heart shall never have a wrinkle in it, so long as I can cry
"Hem," with a clear voice.

HIPPOLITO
You are the happier man, sir.

ORLANDO
Happy man? I'll give you, my lord, the true picture of a happy man; I was turning leaves over this morning, and found it; an excellent Italian painter drew it; if I have it in the right colours, I'll bestow it on your lordship.

HIPPOLITO
I stay for it.

ORLANDO
He that makes gold his wife, but not his whore,
He that at noon-day walks by a prison door,
He that i'th' sun is neither beam nor mote,
He that's not mad after a petticoat,
He for whom poor men's curses dig no grave,

He that is neither lord's nor lawyer's slave,
He that makes this his sea, and that his shore,
He that in's coffin is richer than before,
He that counts youth his sword, and age his staff,
He whose right hand carves his own epitaph,
He that upon his deathbed is a swan,
And dead, no crow—he is a happy man.

HIPPOLITO
It's very well; I thank you for this picture.

ORLANDO
After this picture, my lord, do I strive to have my face drawn: for I am not covetous, am not in debt; sit neither at the duke's side, nor lie at his feet. Wenching and I have done; no man I wrong, no man I fear, no man I fee; I take heed how far I walk, because I know yonder's my home; I would not die like a rich man, to carry nothing away save a winding sheet: but like a good man, to leave Orlando behind me. I sowed leaves in my youth, and I reap now books in my age. I fill this hand, and empty this; and when the bell shall toll for me, if I prove a swan, and go singing to my nest, why so! If a crow! throw me out for carrion, and pick out mine eyes. May not old Friscobaldo, my lord, be merry now! ha?

HIPPOLITO
You may; would I were partner in your mirth.

ORLANDO
I have a little, have all things. I have nothing; I have no wife, I have no child, have no chick; and why should not I be in my jocundare?

HIPPOLITO
Is your wife then departed?

ORLANDO
She's an old dweller in those high countries, yet not from me. Here, she's here: but before me, when a knave and a quean are married, they commonly walk like serjeants together: but a good couple are seldom parted.

HIPPOLITO
You had a daughter too, sir, had you not?

ORLANDO
O my lord! this old tree had one branch, and but one branch growing out of it. It was young, it was fair, it was straight; I pruned it daily, dressed it carefully, kept it from the wind, helped it to the sun, yet for all my skill in planting, it grew crooked, it bore crabs; I hewed it down; what's become of it, I neither know, nor care.

HIPPOLITO
Then I can tell you what's become of it;
That branch is withered.

ORLANDO
So 'twas long ago.

HIPPOLITO
Her name I think was Bellafront, she's dead.

ORLANDO
Ha? dead?

HIPPOLITO
Yes; what of her was left, not worth the keeping,
Even in my sight was thrown into a grave.

ORLANDO
Dead! my last and best peace go with her! I see Death's a good trencherman, he can eat coarse homely meat, as well as the daintiest.

HIPPOLITO
Why, Friscobaldo, was she homely?

ORLANDO
O my lord! a strumpet is one of the devil's vines; all the sins, like so many poles, are stuck upright out of hell, to be her props, that she may spread upon them. And when she's ripe, every slave has a pull at her, then must she be pressed. The young beautiful grape sets the teeth of lust on edge, yet to taste that liquorish wine, is to drink a man's own damnation. Is she dead?

HIPPOLITO
She's turned to earth.

ORLANDO
Would she were turned to Heaven! Umph, is she dead? I am glad the world has lost one of his idols; no whoremonger will at midnight beat at the doors. In her grave sleep all my shame, and her own; and all my sorrows, and all her sins!

HIPPOLITO
I'm glad you're wax, not marble; you are made
Of man's best temper; there are now good hopes
That all these heaps of ice about your heart,
By which a father's love was frozen up,
Are thawed in these sweet showers, fetched from your eyes;
We are ne'er like angels till our passion dies.
She is not dead, but lives under worse fate;
I think she's poor; and more to clip her wings,
Her husband at this hour lies in the jail,
For killing of a man. To save his blood,
Join all your force with mine: mine shall be shown:
The getting of his life preserves your own.

ORLANDO
In my daughter, you will say! does she live then? I am sorry I wasted tears upon a harlot; but the best is I have a handkercher to drink them up, soap can wash them all out again. Is she poor?

HIPPOLITO
Trust me, I think she is.

ORLANDO
Then she's a right strumpet; I ne'er knew any of their trade rich two years together; sieves can hold no water, nor harlots hoard up money; they have too many vents, too many sluices to let it out; taverns, tailors, bawds, panders, fiddlers, swaggerers, fools and knaves do all wait upon a common harlot's trencher: she is the gallipot to which these drones fly, not for love to the pot, but for the sweet sucket[7] within it, her money, her money.

[7] Preserve.

HIPPOLITO
I almost dare pawn my word, her bosom
Gives warmth to no such snakes. When did you see her?

ORLANDO
Not seventeen summers.

HIPPOLITO
Is your hate so old?

ORLANDO
Older; it has a white head, and shall never die till she be buried: her wrongs shall be my bedfellow.

HIPPOLITO
Work yet his life, since in it lives her fame.

ORLANDO
No, let him hang, and half her infamy departs out of the world: I hate him for her; he taught her first to taste poison; I hate her for herself, because she refused my physic.

HIPPOLITO
Nay, but Friscobaldo!—

ORLANDO
I detest her, I defy[8] both, she's not mine, she's—

[8] Renounce.

HIPPOLITO
Hear her but speak.

ORLANDO

I love no mermaids, I'll not be caught with a quail-pipe.[9]

[9] Made use of by fowlers to allure quails.

HIPPOLITO
You're now beyond all reason.

ORLANDO
I am then a beast. Sir, I had rather be a beast, and not dishonour my creation, than be a doting father, and like Time, be the destruction of mine own brood.

HIPPOLITO
Is't dotage to relieve your child, being poor?

ORLANDO
Is't fit for an old man to keep a whore?

HIPPOLITO
'Tis charity too.

ORLANDO
'Tis foolery; relieve her!
Were her cold limbs stretched out upon a bier,
I would not sell this dirt under my nails
To buy her an hour's breath, nor give this hair,
Unless it were to choke her.

HIPPOLITO
Fare you well, for I'll trouble you no more.

ORLANDO
And fare you well, sir.

[Exit HIPPOLITO.]

Go thy ways; we have few lords of thy making, that love wenches for their honesty. 'Las my girl! art thou poor? poverty dwells next door to despair, there's but a wall between them; despair is one of hell's catch-poles; and lest that devil arrest her, I'll to her. Yet she shall not know me; she shall drink of my wealth, as beggars do of running water, freely, yet never know from what fountain's head it flows. Shall a silly bird pick her own breast to nourish her young ones, and can a father see his child starve? That were hard; the pelican does it, and shall not I? Yes, I will victual the camp for her, but it shall be by some stratagem. That knave there, her husband, will be hanged, I fear; I'll keep his neck out of the noose if I can, he shall not know how.

Enter two SERVING-MEN.

How now, knaves? Whither wander you?

1st SERVING-MAN
To seek your worship.

ORLANDO
Stay, which of you has my purse? What money have you about you?

2nd SERVING-MAN
Some fifteen or sixteen pounds, sir.

ORLANDO
Give it me.—[Takes purse.]—I think I have some gold about me; yes, it's well. Leave my lodging at court, and get you home. Come, sir, though I never turned any man out of doors, yet I'll be so bold as to pull your coat over your ears.

[ORLANDO puts on the coat of 1st SERVING-MAN, and gives him in exchange his cloak.

1st SERVING-MAN
What do you mean to do, sir?

ORLANDO
Hold thy tongue, knave, take thou my cloak. I hope I play not the paltry merchant in this bart'ring; bid the steward of my house sleep with open eyes in my absence, and to look to all things. Whatsoever I command by letters to be done by you, see it done. So, does it sit well?

2nd SERVING-MAN.
As if it were made for your worship.

ORLANDO
You proud varlets, you need not be ashamed to wear blue,[10] when your master is one of your fellows. Away! do not see me.

[10] *The common livery of the time.*

BOTH.
This is excellent.

[Exeunt SERVING-MEN.

ORLANDO
I should put on a worse suit, too; perhaps I will. My vizard is on; now to this masque. Say I should shave off this honour of an old man, or tie it up shorter.

Well, I will spoil a good face for once.
My beard being off, how should I look? even like
A winter cuckoo, or unfeathered owl;
Yet better lose this hair, than lose her soul.

[Exit.

SCENE III.—A Room in Candido's House.

CANDIDO, the BRIDE and GUESTS discovered at dinner; PRENTICES waiting on them.

Enter LODOVICO, CAROLO, and ASTOLFO.

CANDIDO
O gentlemen, so late, you are very welcome, pray sit down.

LODOVICO
Carolo, did'st e'er see such a nest of caps?[11]

[11] *In allusion to the caps worn both by traders and their apprentices.*

ASTOLFO
Methinks it's a most civil and most comely sight.

LODOVICO
What does he i'th' middle look like?

ASTOLFO
Troth, like a spire steeple in a country village overpeering so many thatched houses.

LODOVICO
It's rather a long pike-staff against so many bucklers without pikes;[12] they sit for all the world like a pair of organs, and he's the tall great roaring pipe i' th' midst.

[12] *Bucklers formerly had long spikes in their centre.*

ASTOLFO
Ha, ha, ha, ha!

CANDIDO
What's that you laugh at, signors?

LODOVICO
Troth, shall I tell you, and aloud I'll tell it;
We laugh to see, yet laugh we not in scorn,
Amongst so many caps that long hat worn.

1st GUEST
Mine is as tall a felt as any is this day in Milan, and therefore I love it, for the block[13] was cleft out for my head, and fits me to a hair.

[13] *The model for the hat.*

CANDIDO
Indeed you're good observers; it shows strange:
But gentlemen, I pray neither contemn,
Nor yet deride a civil ornament;
I could build so much in the round cap's praise,
That 'bove this high roof, I this flat would raise.

LODOVICO
Prithee, sweet bridegroom, do't.

CANDIDO
So all these guests will pardon me, I'll do't.

GUESTS
With all our hearts.

CANDIDO
Thus, then, in the cap's honour.
To every sex, and state, both nature, time,
The country's laws, yea, and the very clime
Do allot distinct habits; the spruce courtier
Jets[14] up and down in silk: the warrior
Marches in buff, the clown plods on in gray:
But for these upper garments thus I say,
The seaman has his cap, pared without brim;
The gallant's head is feathered, that fits him;
The soldier has his morion, women ha' tires;
Beasts have their head-pieces, and men ha' theirs.

[14] Struts.

LODOVICO
Proceed.

CANDIDO
Each degree has his fashion, it's fit then,
One should be laid by for the citizen,
And that's the cap which you see swells not high,
For caps are emblems of humility.
It is a citizen's badge, and first was worn
By th' Romans; for when any bondman's turn
Came to be made a freeman, thus 'twas said,
He to the cap was called, that is, was made
Of Rome a freeman; but was first close shorn:
And so a citizen's hair is still short worn.

LODOVICO

That close shaving made barbers a company,
And now every citizen uses it.

CANDIDO
Of geometric figures the most rare,
And perfect'st, are the circle and the square;
The city and the school much build upon
These figures, for both love proportion.
The city-cap is square, the scholar's round,
To show that government and learning are
The perfect'st limbs i' th' body of a state:
For without them, all's disproportionate.
If the cap had no honour, this might rear it,
The reverend fathers of the law do wear it.
It's light for summer, and in cold it sits
Close to the skull, a warm house for the wits;
It shows the whole face boldly, 'tis not made
As if a man to look on't were afraid,
Nor like a draper's shop with broad dark shed,
For he's no citizen that hides his head.
Flat caps as proper are to city gowns,
As to armours helmets, or to kings their crowns.
Let then the city-cap by none be scorned,
Since with it princes' heads have been adorned.
If more the round cap's honour you would know,
How would this long gown with this steeple[15] show?

[15] *A tall pointed hat satirized by Stubbes in his Anatomie of Abuses (1538). Probably at this point Candido takes the steeple-like hat worn by the 1st Guest, and puts it on his own head.*

ALL
Ha, ha, ha! most vile, most ugly.

CANDIDO
Pray, signor, pardon me, 'twas done in jest.

BRIDE
A cup of claret wine there.

1st PRENTICE
Wine? yes, forsooth, wine for the bride.

CAROLO
You ha' well set out the cap, sir.

LODOVICO
Nay, that's flat.

CANDIDO
A health!

LODOVICO
Since his cap's round, that shall go round. Be bare,
For in the cap's praise all of you have share.

[They bare their heads and drink. As 1st PRENTICE offers the wine to the BRIDE, she hits him on the lips, breaking the glass.

The BRIDE'S at cuffs.

CANDIDO
Oh, peace, I pray thee, thus far off I stand,
I spied the error of my servants;
She called for claret, and you filled out sack;
That cup give me, 'tis for an old man's back,
And not for hers. Indeed, 'twas but mistaken;
Ask all these else.

GUESTS.
No faith, 'twas but mistaken.

1st PRENTICE
Nay, she took it right enough.

CANDIDO
Good Luke, reach her that glass of claret.
Here mistress bride, pledge me there.

BRIDE
Now I'll none.

[Exit.

CANDIDO
How now?

LODOVICO
Look what your mistress ails.

1st PRENTICE
Nothing, sir, but about filling a wrong glass,—a scurvy trick.

CANDIDO
I pray you, hold your tongue.—My servant there tells me she is not well.

GUESTS.

Step to her, step to her.

LODOVICO
A word with you: do ye hear? This wench, your new wife, will take you down in your wedding shoes, unless you hang her up in her wedding garters.

CANDIDO
How, hang her in her garters?

LODOVICO
Will you be a tame pigeon still? Shall your back be like a tortoise shell, to let carts go over it, yet not to break? This she-cat will have more lives than your last puss had, and will scratch worse, and mouse you worse: look to't.

CANDIDO
What would you have me do, sir?

LODOVICO
What would I have you do? Swear, swagger, brawl, fling! For fighting it's no matter, we ha' had knocking pusses enow already; you know, that a woman was made of the rib of a man, and that rib was crooked. The moral of which is, that a man must, from his beginning be crooked to his wife; be you like an orange to her, let her cut you never so fair, be you sour as vinegar. Will you be ruled by me?

CANDIDO
In any thing that's civil, honest, and just.

LODOVICO
Have you ever a prentice's suit will fit me?

CANDIDO
I have the very same which myself wore.

LODOVICO
I'll send my man for't within this half hour, and within this two hour I'll be your prentice. The hen shall not overcrow the cock; I'll sharpen your spurs.

CANDIDO
It will be but some jest, sir?

LODOVICO
Only a jest: farewell, come, Carolo.

[Exeunt LODOVICO, CAROLO, and ASTOLFO.

GUESTS
We'll take our leaves, sir, too.

CANDIDO

Pray conceit not ill
Of my wife's sudden rising. This young knight,
Sir Lodovico, is deep seen in physic,
And he tells me, the disease called the mother,[16]
Hangs on my wife, it is a vehement heaving
And beating of the stomach, and that swelling
Did with the pain thereof cramp up her arm,
That hit his lips, and brake the glass,—no harm,
It was no harm!

[16] Hysteria.

GUESTS
No, signor, none at all.

CANDIDO
The straightest arrow may fly wide by chance.
But come, we'll close this brawl up in some dance.

[Exeunt.

ACT THE SECOND.

SCENE I.—A Room in Matheo's House.

Enter BELLAFRONT and MATHEO.

BELLAFRONT
O my sweet husband! wert thou in thy grave and art alive again? Oh welcome, welcome!

MATHEO
Dost know me? my cloak, prithee, lay't up. Yes, faith, my winding-sheet was taken out of lavender, to be stuck with rosemary[17]: I lacked but the knot here, or here; yet if I had had it, I should ha' made a wry mouth at the world like a plaice[18]: but sweetest villain, I am here now and I will talk with thee soon.

[17] Rosemary was used as an emblem of remembrance at both funerals and weddings.

[18] A favourite simile with the writers of the time.

BELLAFRONT
And glad am I thou art here.

MATHEO
Did these heels caper in shackles? Ah! my little plump rogue. I'll bear up for all this, and fly high. Catso catso.[19]

[19] Ital. A term of abuse or contempt.

BELLAFRONT
Matheo?

MATHEO
What sayest, what sayest? O brave fresh air! a pox on these grates and gingling of keys, and rattling of iron. I'll bear up, I'll fly high, wench, hang toff.

BELLAFRONT
Matheo, prithee, make thy prison thy glass,
And in it view the wrinkles, and the scars,
By which thou wert disfigured; viewing them, mend them.

MATHEO
I'll go visit all the mad rogues now, and the good roaring boys.[20]

[20] Roystering young gallants. A highly favourable female version of the type is given in Dekker and Middleton's comedy, The Roaring Girl.

BELLAFRONT
Thou dost not hear me?

MATHEO
Yes, faith, do I.

BELLAFRONT
Thou has been in the hands of misery, and ta'en strong physic; prithee now be sound.

MATHEO
Yes. 'Sfoot, I wonder how the inside of a tavern looks now. Oh, when shall I bizzle, bizzle?[21]

[21] i.e. Get a chance of drinking to excess.

BELLAFRONT
Nay, see, thou'rt thirsty still for poison! Come, I will not have thee swagger.

MATHEO
Honest ape's face!

BELLAFRONT
'Tis that sharpened an axe to cut thy throat.
Good love, I would not have thee sell thy substance
And time, worth all, in those damned shops of hell;
Those dicing houses, that stand never well,
But when they stand most ill; that four-squared sin
Has almost lodged us in the beggar's inn.
Besides, to speak which even my soul does grieve,

A sort of ravens have hung upon thy sleeve,
And fed upon thee: good Mat, if you please,
Scorn to spread wing amongst so base as these;
By them thy fame is speckled, yet it shows
Clear amongst them; so crows are fair with crows.
Custom in sin, gives sin a lovely dye;
Blackness in Moors is no deformity.

MATHEO
Bellafront, Bellafront, I protest to thee, I swear, as I hope for my soul, I will turn over a new leaf. The prison I confess has bit me; the best man that sails in such a ship, may be lousy.

[Knocking within.

BELLAFRONT
One knocks at door.

MATHEO
I'll be the porter: they shall see a jail cannot hold a brave spirit, I'll fly high.

[Exit.

BELLAFRONT
How wild is his behaviour! Oh, I fear
He's spoiled by prison, he's half damned comes there,
But I must sit all storms: when a full sail
His fortunes spread, he loved me: being now poor,
I'll beg for him, and no wife can do more.

Re-enter MATHEO, with ORLANDO disguised as a SERVING-MAN.

MATHEO
Come in, pray! would you speak with me, sir?

ORLANDO
Is your name Signor Matheo?

MATHEO
My name is Signor Matheo.

ORLANDO
Is this gentlewoman your wife, sir?

MATHEO
This gentlewoman is my wife, sir.

ORLANDO

The Destinies spin a strong and even thread of both your loves!—The mother's own face, I ha' not forgot that. [Aside.] I'm an old man, sir, and am troubled with a whoreson salt rheum, that I cannot hold my water.—Gentlewoman, the last man I served was your father.

BELLAFRONT
My father? any tongue that sounds his name,
Speaks music to me; welcome, good old man!
How does my father? lives he? has he health?
How does my father?—I so much do shame him,
So much do wound him, that I scarce dare name him. [Aside.

ORLANDO
I can speak no more.

MATHEO
How now, old lad, what dost cry?

ORLANDO
The rheum still, sir, nothing else; I should be well seasoned, for mine eyes lie in brine. Look you, sir, I have a suit to you.

MATHEO
What is't, my little white-pate?

ORLANDO
Troth, sir, I have a mind to serve your worship.

MATHEO
To serve me? Troth, my friend, my fortunes are, as a man may say—

ORLANDO
Nay, look you, sir, I know, when all sins are old in us, and go upon crutches, that covetousness does but then lie in her cradle; 'tis not so with me. Lechery loves to dwell in the fairest lodging, and covetousness in the oldest buildings, that are ready to fall: but my white head, sir, is no inn for such a gossip. If a serving-man at my years, that has sailed about the world, be not stored with biscuit enough to serve him the voyage out of his life, and to bring him East home, ill pity but all his days should be fasting days. I care not so much for wages, for I have scraped a handful of gold together. I have a little money, sir, which I would put into your worship's hands, not so much to make it more—

MATHEO
No, no, you say well, thou sayest well; but I must tell you,—how much is the money, sayest thou?

ORLANDO
About twenty pound, sir.

MATHEO
Twenty pound? Let me see: that shall bring thee in, after ten per centum per annum.

ORLANDO
No, no, no, sir, no: I cannot abide to have money engender: fie upon this silver lechery, fie; if I may have meat to my mouth, and rags to my back, and a flock-bed to snort upon when I die, the longer liver take all.

MATHEO
A good old boy, i'faith! If thou servest me, thou shall eat as I eat, drink as I drink, lie as I lie, and ride as I ride.

ORLANDO
That's if you have money to hire horses. [Aside.

MATHEO
Front, what dost thou think on't? This good old lad here shall serve me.

BELLAFRONT
Alas, Matheo, wilt thou load a back
That is already broke?

MATHEO
Peace, pox on you, peace. There's a trick in't, I fly high, it shall be so, Front, as I tell you: give me thy hand, thou shalt serve me i'faith: welcome: as for your money—

ORLANDO
Nay, look you, sir, I have it here.

MATHEO
Pish, keep it thyself, man, and then thou'rt sure 'tis safe.

ORLANDO
Safe! an' twere ten thousand ducats, your worship should be my cash-keeper; I have heard what your worship is, an excellent dunghill cock, to scatter all abroad; but I'll venture twenty pounds on's head.

[Gives money to MATHEO.

MATHEO
And didst thou serve my worshipful father-in-law, Signor
Orlando Friscobaldo, that madman, once?

ORLANDO
I served him so long, till he turned me out of doors.

MATHEO
It's a notable chuff: I ha' not seen him many a day.

ORLANDO
No matter an you ne'er see him; it's an arrant grandee, a churl, and as damned a cut-throat.

BELLAFRONT
Thou villain, curb thy tongue! thou art a Judas,
To sell thy master's name to slander thus.

MATHEO
Away, ass! He speaks but truth, thy father is a—

BELLAFRONT
Gentleman.

MATHEO
And an old knave. There's more deceit in him than in sixteen 'pothecaries: it's a devil; thou mayest beg, starve, hang, damn! does he send thee so much as a cheese?

ORLANDO
Or so much as a gammon of bacon,
He'll give it his dogs first.

MATHEO
A jail, a jail.

ORLANDO
A Jew, a Jew, sir.

MATHEO
A dog!

ORLANDO
An English mastiff, sir.

MATHEO
Pox rot out his old stinking garbage!

BELLAFRONT
Art not ashamed to strike an absent man thus?
Art not ashamed to let this vile dog bark,
And bite my father thus? I'll not endure it.
Out of my doors, base slave!

MATHEO
Your doors? a vengeance! I shall live to cut that old rogue's throat, for all you take his part thus.

ORLANDO
He shall live to see thee hanged first. [Aside.

Enter HIPPOLITO.

MATHEO

God's-so, my lord, your lordship is most welcome, I'm proud of this, my lord.

HIPPOLITO
Was bold to see you.
Is that your wife?

MATHEO
Yes, sir.

HIPPOLITO
I'll borrow her lip.

[Kisses BELLAFRONT.

MATHEO
With all my heart, my lord.

ORLANDO
Who's this, I pray, sir.

MATHEO
My Lord Hippolito: what's thy name?

ORLANDO
Pacheco.

MATHEO
Pacheco, fine name; thou seest, Pacheco, I keep company with no scoundrels, nor base fellows.

HIPPOLITO
Came not my footman to you?

BELLAFRONT
Yes, my lord.

HIPPOLITO
I sent by him a diamond and a letter,
Did you receive them?

BELLAFRONT
Yes, my lord, I did.

HIPPOLITO
Read you the letter?

BELLAFRONT
O'er and o'er 'tis read.

HIPPOLITO
And, faith, your answer?

BELLAFRONT
Now the time's not fit,
You see, my husband's here.

HIPPOLITO
I'll now then leave you,
And choose mine hour; but ere I part away,
Hark you, remember I must have no nay—
Matheo, I will leave you.

MATHEO
A glass of wine.

HIPPOLITO
Not now, I'll visit you at other times.
You're come off well, then?

MATHEO
Excellent well. I thank your lordship: I owe you my life, my lord; and will pay my best blood in any service of yours.

HIPPOLITO
I'll take no such dear payment. Hark you, Matheo, I know the prison is a gulf. If money run low with you, my purse is your's: call for it.

MATHEO
Faith, my lord, I thank my stars, they send me down some;
I cannot sink, so long these bladders hold.

HIPPOLITO
I will not see your fortunes ebb, pray, try.
To starve in full barns were fond[22] modesty.

[22] Foolish.

MATHEO
Open the door, sirrah.

HIPPOLITO
Drink this, and anon, I pray thee, give thy mistress this.

[Gives to ORLANDO, who opens the door, first money, then a purse, and exit.

ORLANDO
O noble spirit, if no worse guests here dwell,

My blue coat sits on my old shoulders well.

MATHEO
The only royal fellow, he's bounteous as the Indies, what's that he said to thee, Bellafront?

BELLAFRONT
Nothing.

MATHEO
I prithee, good girl?

BELLAFRONT
Why, I tell you, nothing.

MATHEO
Nothing? it's well: tricks! that I must be beholden to a scald hot-livered goatish gallant, to stand with my cap in my hand, and vail bonnet, when I ha' spread as lofty sails as himself. Would I had been hanged. Nothing? Pacheco, brush my cloak.

ORLANDO
Where is't, sir?

MATHEO
Come, we'll fly high.
Nothing? There is a whore still in thy eye.

[Exit.

ORLANDO
My twenty pounds fly high, O wretched woman!
This varlet's able to make Lucrece common. [Aside.
How now, mistress? has my master dyed you into this sad colour?

BELLAFRONT
Fellow, begone I pray thee; if thy tongue
Itch after talk so much, seek out thy master.
Thou'rt a fit instrument for him.

ORLANDO
Zounds, I hope he will not play upon me!

BELLAFRONT
Play on thee? no, you two will fly together,
Because you're roving arrows of one feather.
Would thou wouldst leave my house, thou ne'er shalt please me!
Weave thy nets ne'er so high,
Thou shalt be but a spider in mine eye.
Thou'rt rank with poison, poison tempered well

Is food for health; but thy black tongue doth swell
With venom, to hurt him that gave thee bread:
To wrong men absent, is to spurn the dead.
And so did'st thou my master, and my father.

ORLANDO
You have small reason to take his part; for I have heard him say five hundred times, you were as arrant a whore as ever stiffened tiffany neckcloths in water-starch upon a Saturday i' th' afternoon.

BELLAFRONT
Let him say worse, when for the earth's offence
Hot vengeance through the marble clouds is driven,
Is't fit earth shoot again those darts at heaven?

ORLANDO
And so if your father call you whore you'll not call him old knave:—Friscobaldo, she carries thy mind up and down; she's thine own flesh, blood, and bone. [Aside] Troth, mistress, to tell you true, the fireworks that ran from me upon lines against my good old master, your father, were but to try how my young master, your husband, loved such squibs: but it's well known, I love your father as myself; I'll ride for him at mid-night, run for you by owl-light; I'll die for him, drudge for you; I'll fly low, and I'll fly high, as my master says, to do you good, if you'll forgive me.

BELLAFRONT
I am not made of marble; I forgive thee.

ORLANDO
Nay, if you were made of marble, a good stone-cutter might cut you. I hope the twenty pound I delivered to my master, is in a sure hand.

BELLAFRONT
In a sure hand, I warrant thee, for spending.

ORLANDO
I see my young master is a mad-cap, and a bonus socius. I love him well, mistress: yet as well as I love him, I'll not play the knave with you; look you, I could cheat you of this purse full of money; but I am an old lad, and I scorn to cony-catch[23]: yet I ha' been dog at a cony in my time.

[Gives purse.

[23] *Cheat.*

BELLAFRONT
A purse? where hadst it?

ORLANDO
The gentleman that went away, whispered in mine ear, and charged me to give it you.

BELLAFRONT

The Lord Hippolito?

ORLANDO
Yes, if he be a lord, he gave it me.

BELLAFRONT
'Tis all gold.

ORLANDO
'Tis like so: it may be, he thinks you want money, and therefore bestows his alms bravely, like a lord.

BELLAFRONT
He thinks a silver net can catch the poor;
Here's bait to choke a nun, and turn her whore.
Wilt thou be honest to me?

ORLANDO
As your nails to your fingers, which I think never deceived you.

BELLAFRONT
Thou to this lord shalt go, commend me to him,
And tell him this, the town has held out long,
Because within 'twas rather true than strong.
To sell it now were base; Say 'tis no hold
Built of weak stuff, to be blown up with gold.
He shall believe thee by this token, or this;
If not, by this.

[Giving purse, ring and letters.

ORLANDO
Is this all?

BELLAFRONT
This is all.

ORLANDO
Mine own girl still!   [Aside.

BELLAFRONT
A star may shoot, not fall.

[Exit.

ORLANDO
A star? nay, thou art more than the moon, for thou hast neither changing quarters, nor a man standing in thy circle with a bush of thorns. Is't possible the Lord Hippolito, whose face is as civil as the outside of a dedicatory book, should be a muttonmonger?[24] A poor man has but one ewe, and this grandee

sheep-biter leaves whole flocks of fat wethers, whom he may knock down, to devour this. I'll trust neither lord nor butcher with quick flesh for this trick; the cuckoo, I see now, sings all the year, though every man cannot hear him; but I'll spoil his notes. Can neither love-letters, nor the devil's common pick-locks, gold, nor precious stones make my girl draw up her percullis?[25] Hold out still, wench.

[24] Whoremonger.

[25] Portcullis.

All are not bawds, I see now, that keep doors,
Nor all good wenches that are marked for whores.

[Exit.

SCENE II.—Before Candido's Shop.

Enter CANDIDO, and LODOVICO disguised as a PRENTICE.

LODOVICO
Come, come, come, what do ye lack, sir? what do ye lack, sir? what is't ye lack, sir? Is not my worship well suited? Did you ever see a gentleman better disguised?

CANDIDO
Never, believe me, signor.

LODOVICO
Yes, but when he has been drunk. There be prentices would make mad gallants, for they would spend all, and drink, and whore, and so forth; and I see we gallants could make mad prentices. How does thy wife like me? Nay, I must not be so saucy, then I spoil all: pray you how does my mistress like me?

CANDIDO
Well; for she takes you for a very simple fellow.

LODOVICO
And they that are taken for such are commonly the arrantest knaves: but to our comedy, come.

CANDIDO
I shall not act it; chide, you say, and fret,
And grow impatient: I shall never do't.

LODOVICO
'Sblood, cannot you do as all the world does, counterfeit?

CANDIDO
Were I a painter, that should live by drawing
Nothing but pictures of an angry man,

I should not earn my colours; I cannot do't.

LODOVICO
Remember you're a linen-draper, and that if you give your wife a yard, she'll take an ell: give her not therefore a quarter of your yard, not a nail.

CANDIDO
Say I should turn to ice, and nip her love
Now 'tis but in the bud.

LODOVICO
Well, say she's nipt.

CANDIDO
It will so overcharge her heart with grief,
That like a cannon, when her sighs go off,
She in her duty either will recoil,
Or break in pieces and so die: her death,
By my unkindness might be counted murder.

LODOVICO
Die? never, never. I do not bid you beat her, nor give her black eyes, nor pinch her sides; but cross her humours. Are not baker's arms the scales of justice? yet is not their bread light? and may not you, I pray, bridle her with a sharp bit, yet ride her gently?

CANDIDO
Well, I will try your pills,
Do you your faithful service, and be ready
Still at a pinch to help me in this part,
Or else I shall be out clean.

LODOVICO
Come, come, I'll prompt you.

CANDIDO
I'll call her forth now, shall I?

LODOVICO
Do, do, bravely.

CANDIDO
Luke, I pray, bid your mistress to come hither.

LODOVICO
Luke, I pray, bid your mistress to come hither.

CANDIDO
Sirrah, bid my wife come to me: why, when?[26]

[26] *An expression signifying impatience.*

1st PRENTICE [Within]
Presently, sir, she comes.

LODOVICO
La, you, there's the echo! she comes.

Enter BRIDE.

BRIDE
What is your pleasure with me?

CANDIDO
Marry, wife,
I have intent; and you see this stripling here,
He bears good will and liking to my trade,
And means to deal in linen.

LODOVICO
Yes, indeed, sir, I would deal in linen, if my mistress like me so well as I like her.

CANDIDO
I hope to find him honest, pray; good wife, look that his bed and chamber be made ready.

BRIDE
You're best to let him hire me for his maid.
I look to his bed? look to't yourself.

CANDIDO
Even so?
I swear to you a great oath—

LODOVICO
Swear, cry Zounds!—

CANDIDO
I will not—go to, wife—I will not—

LODOVICO
That your great oath?

CANDIDO
Swallow these gudgeons!

LODOVICO
Well said!

BRIDE
Then fast, then you may choose.

CANDIDO
You know at table
What tricks you played, swaggered, broke glasses, fie!
Fie, fie, fie! and now before my prentice here,
You make an ass of me, thou—what shall I call thee?

BRIDE
Even what you will.

LODOVICO
Call her arrant whore.

CANDIDO
Oh fie, by no means! then she'll call me cuckold.
Sirrah, go look to th' shop. How does this show?

LODOVICO
Excellent well—I'll go look to the shop, sir.
Fine cambrics, lawns; what do you lack?

[Goes into the shop.

CANDIDO
A curst cow's milk I ha' drunk once before,
And 'twas so rank in taste, I'll drink no more.
Wife, I'll tame you.

BRIDE
You may, sir, if you can,
But at a wrestling I have seen a fellow
Limbed like an ox, thrown by a little man.

CANDIDO
And so you'll throw me?—Reach me, knaves, a yard!

LODOVICO
A yard for my master.

[LODOVICO returns from the shop with a yard-wand and followed by PRENRICES.

1st PRENTICE
My master is grown valiant.

CANDIDO

I'll teach you fencing tricks.

PRENTICES
Rare, rare! a prize!

LODOVICO
What will you do, sir?

CANDIDO
Marry, my good prentice, nothing but breathe my wife.

BRIDE
Breathe me with your yard?

LODOVICO
No, he'll but measure you out, forsooth.

BRIDE
Since you'll needs fence, handle your weapon well,
For if you take a yard, I'll take an ell.
Reach me an ell!

LODOVICO
An ell for my mistress! [Brings an ell wand from the shop. Keep the laws of the noble science, sir, and measure weapons with her; your yard is a plain heathenish weapon; 'tis too short, she may give you a handful, and yet you'll not reach her.

CANDIDO
Yet I ha' the longer arm.—Come fall to't roundly,
And spare not me, wife, for I'll lay't on soundly:
If o'er husbands their wives will needs be masters,
We men will have a law to win't at wasters.[27]

[27] Cudgels.

LODOVICO
'Tis for the breeches, is't not?

CANDIDO
For the breeches!

BRIDE
Husband, I'm for you, I'll not strike in jest.

CANDIDO
Nor I.

BRIDE

But will you sign to one request?

CANDIDO
What's that?

BRIDE
Let me give the first blow.

CANDIDO
The first blow, wife? shall I?

LODOVICO
Let her ha't:
If she strike hard, in to her, and break her pate.

CANDIDO
A bargain: strike!

BRIDE
Then guard you from this blow,
For I play all at legs, but 'tis thus low.

[Kneels.

Behold, I'm such a cunning fencer grown,
I keep my ground, yet down I will be thrown
With the least blow you give me: I disdain
The wife that is her husband's sovereign.
She that upon your pillow first did rest,
They say, the breeches wore, which I detest:
The tax which she imposed on you, I abate you;
If me you make your master, I shall hate you.
The world shall judge who offers fairest play;
You win the breeches, but I win the day.

CANDIDO
Thou win'st the day indeed, give me thy hand;
I'll challenge thee no more: my patient breast
Played thus the rebel, only for a jest:
Here's the rank rider, that breaks colts; 'tis he
Can tame the mad folks, and curst wives easily.

BRIDE
Who? your man?

CANDIDO
My man? my master, though his head be bare,
But he's so courteous, he'll put off his hair.

LODOVICO
Nay, if your service be so hot a man cannot keep his hair on, I'll serve you no longer.

[Takes off his false hair.

BRIDE
Is this your schoolmaster?

LODOVICO
Yes, faith, wench, I taught him to take thee down:
I hope thou canst take him down without teaching;
You ha' got the conquest, and you both are friends.

CANDIDO
Bear witness else.

LODOVICO
My prenticeship then ends.

CANDIDO
For the good service you to me have done,
I give you all your years.

LODOVICO
I thank you, master.
I'll kiss my mistress now, that she may say,
My man was bound, and free all in one day.

[Exeunt.

ACT THE THIRD.

SCENE I.—An Apartment in Hippolito's House.

Enter INFELICE, and ORLANDO disguised as a SERVING-MAN.

INFELICE
From whom sayst thou?

ORLANDO
From a poor gentlewoman, madam, whom I serve.

INFELICE
And what's your business?

ORLANDO
This madam: my poor mistress has a waste piece of ground, which is her own by inheritance, and left to her by her mother. There's a lord now that goes about not to take it clean from her, but to enclose it to himself, and to join it to a piece of his lordship's.

INFELICE
What would she have me do in this?

ORLANDO
No more, madam, but what one woman should do for another in such a case. My honourable lord your husband, would do any thing in her behalf, but she had rather put herself into your hands, because you, a woman, may do more with the duke, your father.

INFELICE
Where lies this land?

ORLANDO
Within a stone's cast of this place; my mistress, I think, would be content to let him enjoy it after her decease, if that would serve his turn, so my master would yield too; but she cannot abide to hear that the lord should meddle with it in her lifetime.

INFELICE
Is she then married? why stirs not her husband in it?

ORLANDO
Her husband stirs in it underhand: but because the other is a great rich man, my master is loath to be seen in it too much.

INFELICE
Let her in writing draw the cause at large:
And I will move the duke.

ORLANDO
'Tis set down, madam, here in black and white already: work it so madam, that she may keep her own without disturbance, grievance, molestation, or meddling of any other; and she bestows this purse of gold on your ladyship.

INFELICE
Old man, I'll plead for her, but take no fees:
Give lawyers them, I swim not in that flood;
I'll touch no gold, till I have done her good.

ORLANDO
I would all proctors' clerks were of your mind, I should law more amongst them than I do then; here, madam, is the survey, not only of the manor itself, but of the grange-house, with every meadow, pasture, plough-land, cony-burrow, fish-pond, hedge, ditch, and bush, that stands in it.

[Gives a letter.

INFELICE
My husband's name, and hand and seal at arms
To a love letter? Where hadst thou this writing?

ORLANDO
From the foresaid party, madam, that would keep the foresaid land out of the foresaid lord's fingers.

INFELICE
My lord turned ranger now?

ORLANDO
You're a good huntress, lady; you ha' found your game already: your lord would fain be a ranger, but my mistress requests you to let him run a course in your own park. If you'll not do't for love, then do't for money! she has no white money, but there's gold; or else she prays you to ring him by this token, and so you shall be sure his nose will not be rooting other men's pastures.

[Gives purse and ring.

INFELICE
This very purse was woven with mine own hands;
This diamond on that very night, when he
Untied my virgin girdle, gave I him:
And must a common harlot share in mine?
Old man, to quit thy pains, take thou the gold.

ORLANDO
Not I, madam, old serving-men want no money.

INFELICE
Cupid himself was sure his secretary;
These lines are even the arrows love let flies,
The very ink dropt out of Venus' eyes.

ORLANDO
I do not think, madam, but he fetched off some poet or other for those lines, for they are parlous hawks to fly at wenches.

INFELICE
Here's honied poison! To me he ne'er thus writ;
But lust can set a double edge on wit.

ORLANDO
Nay, that's true, madam, a wench will whet any thing, if it be not too dull.

INFELICE
Oaths, promises, preferments, jewels, gold,
What snares should break, if all these cannot hold?

What creature is thy mistress?

ORLANDO
One of those creatures that are contrary to man; a woman.

INFELICE
What manner of woman?

ORLANDO
A little tiny woman, lower than your ladyship by head and shoulders, but as mad a wench as ever unlaced a petticoat: these things should I indeed have delivered to my lord, your husband.

INFELICE
They are delivered better: why should she
Send back these things?

ORLANDO
'Ware, 'ware, there's knavery.

INFELICE
Strumpets, like cheating gamesters, will not win
At first: these are but baits to draw him in.
How might I learn his hunting hours?

ORLANDO
The Irish footman can tell you all his hunting hours, the park he hunts in, the doe he would strike; that Irish shackatory[28] beats the bush for him, and knows all; he brought that letter, and that ring; he is the carrier.

[28] A hound,—derived from "Shake a Tory."

INFELICE
Knowest thou what other gifts have passed between them?

ORLANDO
Little Saint Patrick knows all.

INFELICE
Him I'll examine presently.

ORLANDO
Not whilst I am here, sweet madam.

INFELICE
Be gone then, and what lies in me command.

[Exit ORLANDO.

Enter BRYAN.

INFELICE
How much cost those satins,
And cloth of silver, which my husband sent by you
To a low gentlewoman yonder?

BRYAN
Faat satins? faat silvers, faat low gentlefolks? Dow pratest dow knowest not what, i'faat, la.

INFELICE
She there, to whom you carried letters.

BRYAN
By dis hand and bod dow saist true, if I did so, oh how?
I know not a letter a' de book i'faat, la.

INFELICE
Did your lord never send you with a ring, sir,
Set with a diamond?

BRYAN
Never, sa crees[29] fa' me, never! he may run at a towsand rings i'faat, and I never hold his stirrup, till he leap into de saddle. By Saint Patrick, madam, I never touch my lord's diamond, nor ever had to do, i'faat, la, with any of his precious stones.

[29] Críosd—Christ.

Enter HIPPOLITO.

INFELICE
Are you so close, you bawd, you pandering slave?

[Strikes BRYAN.

HIPPOLITO
How now? why, Infelice; what's your quarrel?

INFELICE
Out of my sight, base varlet! get thee gone.

HIPPOLITO
Away, you rogue!

BRYAN
Slawne loot,[30] fare de well, fare de well. Ah marragh frofat boddah breen![31]

[Exit.

[30] Irish: *Slán lúitheach—A joyous farewell(?).*

[31] Irish: *As a márach frómhadh bodach bréan—On the morrow of a feast, a clown is a beast.*

HIPPOLITO
What, grown a fighter? prithee, what's the matter?

INFELICE
If you'll needs know, it was about the clock:
How works the day, my lord, pray, by your watch?

HIPPOLITO
Lest you cuff me, I'll tell you presently: I am near two.

INFELICE
How, two? I'm scarce at one.

HIPPOLITO
One of us then goes false.

INFELICE
Then sure 'tis you,
Mine goes by heaven's dial, the sun, and it goes true.

HIPPOLITO
I think, indeed, mine runs somewhat too fast.

INFELICE
Set it to mine at one then.

HIPPOLITO
One? 'tis past:
'Tis past one by the sun.

INFELICE
Faith, then, belike,
Neither your clock nor mine does truly strike;
And since it is uncertain which goes true,
Better be false at one, than false at two.

HIPPOLITO
You're very pleasant, madam.

INFELICE
Yet not merry.

HIPPOLITO

Why, Infelice, what should make you sad?

INFELICE
Nothing, my lord, but my false watch: pray, tell me,—
You see, my clock or yours is out of frame,
Must we upon the workmen lay the blame,
Or on ourselves that keep them?

HIPPOLITO
Faith on both.
He may by knavery spoil them, we by sloth.
But why talk you all riddle thus? I read
Strange comments in those margins of your looks:
Your cheeks of late are like bad printed books,
So dimly charactered, I scarce can spell
One line of love in them. Sure all's not well.

INFELICE
All is not well indeed, my dearest lord;
Lock up thy gates of hearing, that no sound
Of what I speak may enter.

HIPPOLITO
What means this?

INFELICE
Or if my own tongue must myself betray,
Count it a dream, or turn thine eyes away,
And think me not thy wife.

[Kneels.

HIPPOLITO
Why do you kneel?

INFELICE
Earth is sin's cushion: when the sick soul feels
Herself growing poor, then she turns beggar, cries,
And kneels for help: Hippolito, for husband
I dare not call thee, I have stolen that jewel
Of my chaste honour, which was only thine,
And given it to a slave.

HIPPOLITO
Ha?

INFELICE
On thy pillow

Adultery and lust have slept, thy groom
Hath climbed the unlawful tree, and plucked the sweets,
A villain hath usurped a husband's sheets.

HIPPOLITO
S'death, who?—a cuckold!—who?

INFELICE
This Irish footman.

HIPPOLITO
Worse than damnation! a wild kerne,[32] a frog,
A dog: whom I'll scarce spurn. Longed you for shamrock?
Were it my father's father, heart, I'll kill him,
Although I take him on his death-bed gasping
'Twixt Heaven and hell! a shag-haired cur! Bold strumpet,
Why hang'st thou on me? think'st I'll be a bawd
To a whore, because she's noble?

[32] *A rough sturdy fellow. Irish: Ceithearneach—A soldier.*

INFELICE
I beg but this,
Set not my shame out to the world's broad eye,
Yet let thy vengeance, like my fault, soar high,
So it be in darkened clouds.

HIPPOLITO
Darkened! my horns
Cannot be darkened, nor shall my revenge.
A harlot to my slave? the act is base,
Common, but foul, so shall not thy disgrace.
Could not I feed your appetite? O women
You were created angels, pure and fair;
But since the first fell, tempting devils you are,
You should be men's bliss, but you prove their rods:
Were there no women, men might live like gods;
You ha' been too much down already; rise,
Get from my sight, and henceforth shun my bed;
I'll with no strumpet's breath be poisonèd.
As for your Irish lubrican, that spirit
Whom by preposterous charms thy lust hath raised
In a wrong circle, him I'll damn more black
Then any tyrant's soul.

INFELICE
Hippolito!

HIPPOLITO
Tell me, didst thou bait hooks to draw him to thee,
Or did he bewitch thee?

INFELICE
The slave did woo me.

HIPPOLITO
Tu-whoos in that screech-owl's language. Oh, who'd trust
Your cork-heeled sex? I think to sate your lust,
You'd love a horse, a bear, a croaking toad,
So your hot itching veins might have their bound:
Then the wild Irish dart[33] was thrown? Come, how?
The manner of this fight?

[33] *An allusion to the darts carried by the Irish running footmen.—Dyce.*

INFELICE
'Twas thus, he gave me this battery first.—Oh, I
Mistake—believe me, all this in beaten gold;
Yet I held out, but at length thus was charmed.

[*Gives letter, purse and ring.*

What? change your diamond, wench, the act is base,
Common, but foul, so shall not your disgrace:
Could not I feed your appetite? O men,
You were created angels, pure and fair,
But since the first fell, worse than devils you are.
You should our shields be, but you prove our rods.
Were there no men, women might live like gods.
Guilty, my lord?

HIPPOLITO
Yes, guilty my good lady.

INFELICE
Nay, you may laugh, but henceforth shun my bed,
With no whore's leavings I'll be poisonèd.

[*Exit.*

HIPPOLITO
O'er-reached so finely? 'Tis the very diamond
And letter which I sent: this villany
Some spider closely weaves, whose poisonèd bulk
I must let forth. Who's there without?

SERVING-MAN [Within.]
My lord calls?

HIPPOLITO
Send me the footman.

SERVING-MAN [Within.]
Call the footman to my lord,—Bryan,
Bryan!

HIPPOLITO
It can be no man else, that Irish Judas,
Bred in a country where no venom prospers
But in the nation's blood, hath thus betrayed me.

Re-enter BRYAN.

Slave, get you from your service.

BRYAN
Faat meanest thou by this now?

HIPPOLITO
Question me not, nor tempt my fury, villain
Couldst thou turn all the mountains in the land,
To hills of gold, and give me: here thou stayest not.

BRYAN
I'faat, I care not.

HIPPOLITO
Prate not, but get thee gone, I shall send else.

BRYAN
Ay, do predy, I had rather have thee make a scabbard of my guts, and let out all de Irish puddings in my poor belly, den to be a false knave to de, i'faat! I will never see dine own sweet face more. A mawhid deer a gra,[34] fare dee well, fare dee well; I will go steal cows again in Ireland.

[Exit.

[34] Irish: Maighisdir mo grádh—Master of my love.

HIPPOLITO
He's damned that raised this whirlwind, which hath blown
Into her eyes this jealousy: yet I'll on,
I'll on, stood armed devils staring in my face,
To be pursued in flight, quickens the race,
Shall my blood-streams by a wife's lust be barred?

Fond[35] woman, no: iron grows by strokes more hard;
Lawless desires are seas scorning all bounds,
Or sulphur, which being rammed up, more confounds,
Struggling with madmen madness nothing tames,
Winds wrestling with great fires incense the flames.

[Exit.

[35] Foolish.

SCENE II.—A Room in Matheo's House.

Enter BELLAFRONT, and ORLANDO disguised as a SERVING-MAN.

BELLAFRONT
How now, what ails your master?

ORLANDO
Has taken a younger brother's purge, forsooth, and that
works with him.

BELLAFRONT
Where is his cloak and rapier?

ORLANDO
He has given up his cloak, and his rapier is bound to the peace: If you look a little higher, you may see that another hath entered into hatband for him too. Six and four have put him into this sweat.

BELLAFRONT
Where's all his money?

ORLANDO
'Tis put over by exchange; his doublet was going to be translated, but for me. If any man would ha' lent but half a ducat on his beard, the hair of it had stuffed a pair of breeches by this time; I had but one poor penny, and that I was glad to niggle out, and buy a holly-wand to grace him through the street. As hap was, his boots were on, and them I dustied, to make people think he had been riding, and I had run by him.

BELLAFRONT
Oh me!

Enter MATHEO.

How does my sweet Matheo?

MATHEO

Oh rogue, of what devilish stuff are these dice made of,—the parings of the devil's corns of his toes, that they run thus damnably?

BELLAFRONT
I prithee, vex not.

MATHEO
If any handicraft's-man was ever suffered to keep shop in hell, it will be a dice-maker; he's able to undo more souls than the devil; I played with mine own dice, yet lost. Ha' you any money?

BELLAFRONT
'Las, I ha' none.

MATHEO
Must have money, must have some, must have a cloak, and rapier, and things. Will you go set your lime-twigs, and get me some birds, some money?

BELLAFRONT
What lime-twigs should I set?

MATHEO
You will not then? Must have cash and pictures, do ye hear, frailty? shall I walk in a Plymouth cloak,[36] that's to say, like a rogue, in my hose and doublet, and a crabtree cudgel in my hand, and you swim in your satins? Must have money, come!

[Taking off her gown.

[36] i.e. With a staff.

ORLANDO
Is't bed-time, master, that you undo my mistress?

BELLAFRONT
Undo me? Yes, yes, at these riflings I
Have been too often.

MATHEO
Help to flay, Pacheco.

ORLANDO
Flaying call you it?

MATHEO
I'll pawn you, by th' lord, to your very eyebrows.

BELLAFRONT
With all my heart, since Heaven will have me poor,
As good be drowned at sea, as drowned at shore.

ORLANDO
Why, hear you, sir? i'faith do not make away her gown.

MATHEO
Oh! it's summer, it's summer; your only fashion for a woman now is to be light, to be light.

ORLANDO
Why, pray sir, employ some of that money you have of mine.

MATHEO
Thine? I'll starve first, I'll beg first; when I touch a penny of that, let these fingers' ends rot.

ORLANDO
So they may, for that's past touching. I saw my twenty pounds fly high. [Aside.

MATHEO
Knowest thou never a damned broker about the city?

ORLANDO
Damned broker? yes, five hundred.

MATHEO
The gown stood me in above twenty ducats, borrow ten of it. Cannot live without silver.

ORLANDO
I'll make what I can of it, sir, I'll be your broker,—
But not your damned broker: Oh thou scurvy knave!
What makes a wife turn whore, but such a slave?

[Aside and exit with BELLAFRONT'S gown.

MATHEO
How now, little chick, what ailest, weeping for a handful of tailor's shreds? pox on them, are there not silks enow at mercer's?

BELLAFRONT
I care not for gay feathers, I.

MATHEO
What dost care for then? why dost grieve?

BELLAFRONT
Why do I grieve? A thousand sorrows strike
At one poor heart, and yet it lives. Matheo,
Thou art a gamester, prithee, throw at all,
Set all upon one cast. We kneel and pray,
And struggle for life, yet must be cast away.

Meet misery quickly then, split all, sell all,
And when thou'st sold all, spend it; but I beseech thee
Build not thy mind on me to coin thee more,
To get it wouldst thou have me play the whore?

MATHEO
'Twas your profession before I married you.

BELLAFRONT
Umh? it was indeed: if all men should be branded
For sins long since laid up, who could be saved?
The quarter-day's at hand, how will you do
To pay the rent, Matheo?

MATHEO
Why? do as all of our occupation do against quarter-days: break up house, remove, shift your lodgings: pox a' your quarters!

Enter LODOVICO.

LODOVICO
Where's this gallant?

MATHEO
Signor Lodovico? how does my little Mirror of
Knighthood?[37] this is kindly done i'faith: welcome, by my troth.

[37] An allusion to the well-known romance of this name, from the Spanish.

LODOVICO
And how dost, frolic?—Save you fair lady.—
Thou lookest smug and bravely, noble Mat.

MATHEO
Drink and feed, laugh and lie warm.

LODOVICO
Is this thy wife?

MATHEO
A poor gentlewoman, sir, whom I make use of a'nights.

LODOVICO
Pay custom to your lips, sweet lady.

[Kisses her.

MATHEO

Borrow some shells[38] of him—some wine, sweetheart.

[38] A cant term for money.

LODOVICO
I'll send for't then, i'faith.

MATHEO
You send for't?—Some wine, I prithee.

BELLAFRONT
I ha' no money.

MATHEO
'Sblood, nor I.—What wine love you, signor?

LODOVICO
Here! (Offering money,) or I'll not stay, I protest; trouble the gentlewoman too much?

[Gives money to BELLAFRONT, who goes out.

And what news flies abroad, Matheo?

MATHEO
Troth, none. Oh signor, we ha' been merry in our days.

LODOVICO
And no doubt shall again.
The divine powers never shoot darts at men
Mortal, to kill them.

MATHEO
You say true.

LODOVICO
Why should we grieve at want? Say the world made thee
Her minion, that thy head lay in her lap,
And that she danced thee on her wanton knee,
She could but give thee a whole world: that's all,
And that all's nothing; the world's greatest part
Cannot fill up one corner of thy heart.
Say three corners were all filled, alas!
Of what art thou possessed, a thin blown glass:
Such as is by boys puffed into the air.
Were twenty kingdoms thine, thou'dst live in care:
Thou couldst not sleep the better, nor live longer,
Nor merrier be, nor healthfuller, nor stronger.
If, then, thou want'st, thus make that want thy pleasure,

No man wants all things, nor has all in measure.

MATHEO
I am the most wretched fellow: sure some left-handed priest hath christened me, I am so unlucky; I am never out of one puddle or another; still falling.

Re-enter BELLAFRONT with wine.

Fill out wine to my little finger.
With my heart, i'faith.

[Drinks.

LODOVICO
Thanks, good Matheo.
To your own sweet self.

[Drinks.

Re-enter ORLANDO.

ORLANDO
All the brokers' hearts, sir, are made of flint. I can with all my knocking strike but six sparks of fire out of them; here's six ducats, if you'll take them.

MATHEO
Give me them!

[Taking money.]

An evil conscience gnaw them all! moths and plagues hang upon their lousy wardrobes!

LODOVICO
Is this your man, Matheo?

MATHEO
An old serving-man.

ORLANDO
You may give me t'other half too, sir, that's the beggar.

LODOVICO
What hast there,—gold?

MATHEO
A sort of rascals are in my debt, God knows what, and they feed me with bits, with crumbs, a pox choke them.

LODOVICO
A word, Matheo; be not angry with me;
Believe it that I know the touch of time,
And can part copper though it be gilded o'er,
From the true gold: the sails which thou dost spread,
Would show well if they were not borrowèd.
The sound of thy low fortunes drew me hither,
I give my self unto thee; prithee, use me,
I will bestow on you a suit of satin,
And all things else to fit a gentleman,
Because I love you.

MATHEO
Thanks, good, noble knight!

LODOVICO
Call on me when you please; till then farewell.

[Exit.

MATHEO
Hast angled? hast cut up this fresh salmon?

BELLAFRONT
Wouldst have me be so base?

MATHEO
It's base to steal, its base to be a whore:
Thou'lt be more base, I'll make thee keep a door.[39]

[Exit.

[39] i.e. Turn bawd.

ORLANDO
I hope he will not sneak away with all the money, will he?

BELLAFRONT
Thou sees't he does.

ORLANDO
Nay then, it's well. I set my brains upon an upright last; though my wits be old, yet they are like a withered pippin, wholesome. Look you, mistress, I told him I had but six ducats of the knave broker, but I had eight, and kept these two for you.

BELLAFRONT
Thou should'st have given him all.

ORLANDO
What, to fly high?

BELLAFRONT
Like waves, my misery drives on misery.

[Exit.

ORLANDO
Sell his wife's clothes from her back? does any poulterer's wife pull chickens alive? He riots all abroad, wants all at home: he dices, whores, swaggers, swears, cheats, borrows, pawns: I'll give him hook and line, a little more for all this;

Yet sure i'th end he'll delude all my hopes,
And show me a French trick danced on the ropes.

[Exit.

SCENE III.—Before Candido's Shop.

CANDIDO and his BRIDE discovered in the Shop.

Enter at one side LODOVICO and CAROLO; at another BOTS, and Mistress HORSELEECH.

LODOVICO
Hist, hist, Lieutenant Bots, how dost, man?

CAROLO
Whither are you ambling, Madam Horseleech?

Mistress HORSELEECH
About worldly profit, sir: how do your worships?

BOTS
We want tools, gentlemen, to furnish the trade: they wear out day and night, they wear out till no metal be left in their back. We hear of two or three new wenches are come up with a carrier, and your old goshawk here is flying at them.

LODOVICO
And, faith, what flesh have you at home?

Mistress HORSELEECH
Ordinary dishes; by my troth, sweet men, there's few good i' th' city; I am as well furnished as any, and, though I say it, as well customed.

BOTS

We have meats of all sorts of dressing; we have stewed meat for your Frenchman, pretty light picking meat for your Italian, and that which is rotten roasted for Don Spaniardo.

LODOVICO
A pox on't.

BOTS
We have poulterer's ware for your sweet bloods, as dove, chicken, duck, teal, woodcock, and so forth; and butcher's meat for the citizen: yet muttons[40] fall very bad this year.

[40] Prostitutes.

LODOVICO
Stay, is not that my patient linen-draper yonder, and my fine young smug mistress, his wife?

CAROLO
Sirrah, grannam, I'll give thee for thy fee twenty crowns, if thou canst but procure me the wearing of yon velvet cap.

Mistress HORSELEECH
You'd wear another thing besides the cap. You're a wag.

BOTS
Twenty crowns? we'll share, and I'll be your pully to draw her on.

LODOVICO
Do't presently; we'll ha' some sport.

Mistress HORSELEECH
Wheel you about, sweet men: do you see? I'll cheapen wares of the man, whilst Bots is doing with his wife.

LODOVICO
To't: if we come into the shop to do you grace, we'll call you madam.

BOTS
Pox a' your old face, give it the badge of all scurvy faces, a mask.

[MISTRESS HORSELEECH puts on a mask.

CANDIDO
What is't you lack, gentlewoman? Cambric or lawns, or fine hollands? Pray draw near, I can sell you a pennyworth.

BOTS
Some cambric for my old lady.

CANDIDO

Cambric? you shall, the purest thread in Milan.

CAROLO
Save you, Signor Candido.

LODOVICO
How does my noble master? how my fair mistress?

CANDIDO
My worshipful good servant.—View it well, for 'tis both fine and even.

[Shows cambric.

CAROLO
Cry you mercy, madam; though masked, I thought it should be you by your man.—Pray, signor, show her the best, for she commonly deals for good ware.

CANDIDO
Then this shall fit her.—This is for your ladyship.

BOTS
A word, I pray; there is a waiting gentlewoman of my lady's: her name is Ruyna, says she's your kinswoman, and that you should be one of her aunts.

BRIDE
One of her aunts? troth, sir, I know her not.

BOTS
If it please you to bestow the poor labour of your legs at any time, I will be your convoy thither?

BRIDE
I am a snail, sir, seldom leave my house. If't please her to visit me, she shall be welcome.

BOTS
Do you hear? the naked truth is; my lady hath a young knight, her son, who loves you, you're made, if you lay hold upon't; this jewel he sends you. [Offers jewel.

BRIDE
Sir, I return his love and jewel with scorn; let go my hand, or I shall call my husband. You are an arrant knave.

[Exit.

LODOVICO
What will she do?

BOTS

Do? They shall all do if Bots sets upon them once: she was as if she had professed the trade, squeamish at first; at last I showed her this jewel, said a knight sent it her.

LODOVICO
Is't gold, and right stones?

BOTS
Copper, copper, I go a fishing with these baits. She nibbled, but would not swallow the hook, because the conger-head, her husband, was by; but she bids the gentleman name any afternoon, and she'll meet him at her garden house,[41] which I know.

[41] *Gardens with summer-houses were very common in the suburbs of London at the time, and were often used as places of intrigue.—Dyce.*

LODOVICO
Is this no lie now?

BOTS
Damme, if—

LODOVICO
Oh, prithee stay there.

BOTS
The twenty crowns, sir.

LODOVICO
Before he has his work done? but on my knightly word he shall pay't thee.

Enter ASTOLFO, BERALDO, FONTINELL, and BRYAN.

ASTOLFO
I thought thou hadst been gone into thine own country.

BRYAN
No, faat, la, I cannot go dis four or tree days.

BERALDO
Look thee, yonder's the shop, and that's the man himself.

FONTINELL
Thou shalt but cheapen, and do as we told thee, to put a jest upon him, to abuse his patience.

BRYAN
I'faat, I doubt my pate shall be knocked: but, sa crees sa' me, for your shakes, I will run to any linen-draper in hell: come predee.

ASTOLFO, BERALDO, FONTINELL

Save you, gallants.

LODOVICO, CAROLO
Oh, well met!

CANDIDO
You'll give no more, you say? I cannot take it.

Mistress HORSELEECH
Truly I'll give no more.

CANDIDO
It must not fetch it.
What would you have, sweet gentlemen.

ASTOLFO
Nay, here's the customer.

[Exeunt BOTS and Mistress HORSELEECH.

LODOVICO
The garden-house, you say? we'll bolt[42] out your roguery.

[42] Sift.

CANDIDO
I will but lay these parcels by—my men
Are all at the custom house unloading wares,
If cambric you would deal in, there's the best,
All Milan cannot sample it.

LODOVICO
Do your hear it? one, two, three,—'Sfoot, there came in four gallants! Sure your wife is slipt up, and the fourth man, I hold my life, is grafting your warden tree.[43]

[43] Pear-tree.

CANDIDO
Ha, ha, ha! you gentlemen are full of jest.
If she be up, she's gone some wares to show;
I have above as good wares as below.

LODOVICO
Have you so? nay, then—

CANDIDO
Now, gentlemen, is't cambrics?

BRYAN
I predee now let me have de best waures.

CANDIDO
What's that he says, pray, gentlemen?

LODOVICO
Marry, he says we are like to have the best wars.

CANDIDO
The best wars? all are bad, yet wars do good,
And, like to surgeons, let sick kingdom's blood.

BRYAN
Faat a devil pratest tow so? a pox on dee! I preddee, let me see some hollen, to make linen shirts, for fear my body be lousy.

CANDIDO
Indeed, I understand no word he speaks.

CAROLO
Marry, he says that at the siege in Holland
There was much bawdry used among the soldiers,
Though they were lousy.

CANDIDO
It may be so, that likely; true, indeed,
In every garden, sir, does grow that weed.

BRYAN
Pox on de gardens, and de weeds, and de fool's cap dere, and de clouts! hear? dost make a hobby-horse of me?

[Tearing the cambric.

ALL
Oh, fie! he has torn the cambric.

CANDIDO
'Tis no matter.

ASTOLFO
It frets me to the soul.

CANDIDO
So does't not me.
My customers do oft for remnants call,
These are two remnants, now, no loss at all.

But let me tell you, were my servants here,
It would ha' cost more.—Thank you, gentlemen,
I use you well, pray know my shop again.

ALL
Ha, ha, ha! come, come, let's go, let's go.

[Exeunt.

ACT THE FOURTH.

SCENE I.—A Room in Matheo's House.

Enter MATHEO brave,[44] and BELLAFRONT.

[44] Finely attired.

MATHEO
How am I suited, Front? am I not gallant, ha?

BELLAFRONT
Yes, sir, you are suited well.

MATHEO
Exceeding passing well, and to the time.

BELLAFRONT
The tailor has played his part with you.

MATHEO
And I have played a gentleman's part with my tailor, for
I owe him for the making of it.

BELLAFRONT
And why did you so, sir?

MATHEO
To keep the fashion; it's your only fashion now, of your best rank of gallants, to make their tailors wait for their money; neither were it wisdom indeed to pay them upon the first edition of a new suit; for commonly the suit is owing for, when the linings are worn out, and there's no reason, then, that the tailor should be paid before the mercer.

BELLAFRONT
Is this the suit the knight bestowed upon you?

MATHEO

This is the suit, and I need not shame to wear it, for better men than I would be glad to have suits bestowed on them. It's a generous fellow,—but—pox on him—we whose pericranions are the very limbecks and stillatories of good wit and fly high, must drive liquor out of stale gaping oysters—shallow knight, poor squire Tinacheo: I'll make a wild Cataian[45] of forty such: hang him, he's an ass, he's always sober.

[45] *A Cataian came to signify a sharper because the people of Cataia (China) were famous for their thieving propensities.—Dyce.*

BELLAFRONT
This is your fault to wound your friends still.

MATHEO
No, faith, Front, Lodovico is a noble Slavonian: it's more rare to see him in a woman's company, than for a Spaniard to go into England, and to challenge the English fencers there.—[Knocking within.] One knocks,—see.—

[Exit BELLAFRONT.]

—La, fa, fol, la, fa, la, [Sings] rustle in silks and satins! there's music in this, and a taffeta petticoat, it makes both fly high. Catso.

Re-enter BELLAFRONT with ORLANDO in his, own dress, and four SERVANTS.

BELLAFRONT
Matheo! 'tis my father.

MATHEO
Ha! father? It's no matter, he finds no tattered prodigals here.

ORLANDO
Is not the door good enough to hold your blue coats?[46] away, knaves, Wear not your clothes threadbare at knees for me; beg Heaven's blessing, not mine.—

[Exeunt SERVANTS.]

—Oh cry your worship mercy, sir; was somewhat bold to talk to this gentlewoman, your wife here.

[46] *Serving-men's livery at this time was usually blue.*

MATHEO
A poor gentlewoman, sir.

ORLANDO
Stand not, sir, bare to me; I ha' read oft
That serpents who creep low, belch ranker poison
Than wingèd dragons do that fly aloft.

MATHEO
If it offend you, sir, 'tis for my pleasure.

ORLANDO
Your pleasure be't, sir. Umh, is this your palace?

BELLAFRONT
Yes, and our kingdom, for 'tis our content.

ORLANDO
It's a very poor kingdom then; what, are all your subjects gone a sheep-shearing? not a maid? not a man? not so much as a cat? You keep a good house belike, just like one of your profession, every room with bare walls, and a half-headed bed to vault upon, as all your bawdy-houses are. Pray who are your upholsters? Oh, the spiders, I see, they bestow hangings upon you.

MATHEO
Bawdy-house? Zounds, sir—

BELLAFRONT
Oh sweet Matheo, peace. Upon my knees
I do beseech you, sir, not to arraign me
For sins, which Heaven, I hope, long since hath pardoned!
Those flames, like lightning flashes, are so spent,
The heat no more remains, than where ships went,
Or where birds cut the air, the print remains.

MATHEO
Pox on him, kneel to a dog.

BELLAFRONT
She that's a whore,
Lives gallant, fares well, is not, like me, poor.
I ha' now as small acquaintance with that sin,
As if I had never known't, t' had never been.

ORLANDO
No acquaintance with it? what maintains thee then? how dost live then? Has thy husband any lands? any rents coming in, any stock going, any ploughs jogging, any ships sailing? hast thou any wares to turn, so much as to get a single penny by?

Yes thou hast ware to sell,
Knaves are thy chapmen, and thy shop is hell.

MATHEO
Do you hear, sir?

ORLANDO
So, sir, I do hear, sir, more of you than you dream I do.

MATHEO
You fly a little too high, sir.

ORLANDO
Why, sir, too high?

MATHEO
I ha' suffered your tongue, like a bard cater-tray,[47] to run all this while, and ha' not stopt it.

[47] A kind of false dice.

ORLANDO
Well, sir, you talk like a gamester.

MATHEO
If you come to bark at her, because she's a poor rogue, look you, here's a fine path, sir, and there, there's the door.

BELLAFRONT
Matheo?

MATHEO
Your blue coats stay for you, sir. I love a good honest roaring boy, and so—

ORLANDO
That's the devil.

MATHEO
Sir, sir, I'll ha' no Joves in my house to thunder avaunt: she shall live and be maintained when you, like a keg of musty sturgeon, shall stink; where? in your coffin—how? be a musty fellow, and lousy.

ORLANDO
I know she shall be maintained, but how? she like a quean, thou like a knave; she like a whore, thou like a thief.

MATHEO
Thief? Zounds! Thief?

BELLAFRONT
Good, dearest Mat!—Father!

MATHEO
Pox on you both! I'll not be braved. New satin scorns to be put down with bare bawdy velvet. Thief?

ORLANDO
Ay, thief, th'art a murderer, a cheater, a whoremonger, a pot-hunter, a borrower a beggar—

BELLAFRONT
Dear father—

MATHEO
An old ass, a dog, a churl, a chuff, an usurer, a villain, a moth, a mangy mule, with an old velvet foot-cloth on his back, sir.

BELLAFRONT
Oh me!

ORLANDO
Varlet, for this I'll hang thee.

MATHEO
Ha, ha, alas!

ORLANDO
Thou keepest a man of mine here, under my nose—

MATHEO
Under thy beard.

ORLANDO
As arrant a smell-smock, for an old muttonmonger[48] as thyself.

[48] Whoremonger.

MATHEO
No, as yourself.

ORLANDO
As arrant a purse-taker as ever cried, Stand! yet a good fellow I confess, and valiant; but he'll bring thee to th' gallows; you both have robbed of late two poor country pedlars.

MATHEO
How's this? how's this? dost thou fly high? Rob pedlars?—bear witness, Front—rob pedlars? my man and I a thief?

BELLAFRONT
Oh, sir, no more.

ORLANDO
Ay, knave, two pedlars; hue and cry is up; warrants are out, and I shall see thee climb a ladder.

MATHEO
And come down again as well as a bricklayer or a tiler. How the vengeance knows he this? If I be hanged, I'll tell the people I married old Friscobaldo's daughter; I'll frisco you, and your old carcass.

ORLANDO
Tell what you canst; if I stay here longer, I shall be hanged too, for being in thy company; therefore, as I found you, I leave you—

MATHEO
Kneel, and get money of him.

ORLANDO
A knave and a quean, a thief and a strumpet, a couple of beggars, a brace of baggages.

MATHEO
Hang upon him—Ay, ay, sir, farewell; we are—follow close—we are beggars—in satin—to him.

BELLAFRONT
Is this your comfort, when so many years
You ha' left me frozen to death?

ORLANDO
Freeze still, starve still!

BELLAFRONT
Yes, so I shall: I must: I must and will.
If as you say I'm poor, relieve me then,
Let me not sell my body to base men.
You call me strumpet, Heaven knows I am none:
Your cruelty may drive me to be one:
Let not that sin be yours; let not the shame
Of common whore live longer than my name.
That cunning bawd, necessity, night and day
Plots to undo me; drive that hag away,
Lest being at lowest ebb, as now I am,
I sink for ever.

ORLANDO
Lowest ebb, what ebb?

BELLAFRONT
So poor, that, though to tell it be my shame,
I am not worth a dish to hold my meat;
I am yet poorer, I want bread to eat.

ORLANDO
It's not seen by your cheeks.

MATHEO
I think she has read an homily to tickle the old rogue. [Aside.

ORLANDO

Want bread! there's satin: bake that.

MATHEO
'Sblood, make pasties of my clothes?

ORLANDO
A fair new cloak, stew that; an excellent gilt rapier.

MATHEO
Will you eat that, sir?

ORLANDO
I could feast ten good fellows with these hangers.[49]

[49] *The loops or straps appended to the girdle in which the dagger or small sword usually hung.—Halliwell.*

MATHEO
The pox, you shall!

ORLANDO
I shall not, till thou begg'st, think thou art poor;
And when thou begg'st I'll feed thee at my door,
As I feed dogs, with bones; till then beg, borrow,
Pawn, steal, and hang, turn bawd, when th'art whore.—
My heart-strings sure would crack, were they strained more.

[Aside, and exit.

MATHEO
This is your father, your damned—Confusion light upon all the generation of you; he can come bragging hither with four white herrings at's tail in blue coats, without roes in their bellies, but I may starve ere he give me so much as a cob.[50]

[50] *Means both a herring and a piece of money.*

BELLAFRONT
What tell you me of this? alas!

MATHEO
Go, trot after your dad, do you capitulate; I'll pawn not for you; I'll not steal to be hanged for such an hypocritical, close, common harlot: away, you dog!—Brave i'faith! Udsfoot, give me some meat.

BELLAFRONT
Yes, sir.

[Exit.

MATHEO
Goodman slave, my man too, is galloped to the devil a' t'other side: Pacheco, I'll checo you. Is this your dad's day? England, they say, is the only hell for horses, and only paradise for women: pray get you to that paradise, because you're called an honest whore; there they live none but honest whores with a pox. Marry here in our city, all your sex are but foot-cloth nags,[51] the master no sooner lights but the man leaps into the saddle.

[51] *Horses with long housings.*

Re-enter BELLAFRONT with meat and drink.

BELLAFRONT
Will you sit down I pray, sir?

MATHEO
[Sitting down.] I could tear, by th' Lord, his flesh, and eat his midriff in salt, as I eat this:—must I choke—my father Friscobaldo, I shall make a pitiful hog-louse of you, Orlando, if you fall once into my fingers—Here's the savourest meat! I ha' got a stomach with chafing. What rogue should tell him of those two pedlars? A plague choke him, and gnaw him to the bare bones!—Come fill.

BELLAFRONT
Thou sweatest with very anger, good sweet, vex not, as 'tis no fault of mine.

MATHEO
Where didst buy this mutton? I never felt better ribs.

BELLAFRONT
A neighbour sent it me.

Re-enter ORLANDO disguised as a SERVING-MAN.

MATHEO
Hah, neighbour? foh, my mouth stinks,—You whore, do you beg victuals for me? Is this satin doublet to be bombasted[52] with broken meat?

[Takes up the stool.

[52] *Stuffed out.*

ORLANDO
What will you do, sir?

MATHEO
Beat out the brains of a beggarly—

ORLANDO
Beat out an ass's head of your own—Away, Mistress

[Exit BELLAFRONT.]

Zounds, do but touch one hair of her, and I'll so quilt your cap with old iron, that your coxcomb shall ache like a roasted rabbit, that you must have the head for the brains?

MATHEO
Ha, ha! go out of my doors, you rogue, away, four marks; trudge.

ORLANDO
Four marks? no, sir, my twenty pound that you ha' made fly high, and I am gone.

MATHEO
Must I be fed with chippings? you're best get a clapdish,[53] and say you're proctor to some spittle-house.[54] Where hast thou been, Pacheco? Come hither my little turkey-cock.

[53] The clap or clack-dish was properly a box carried by beggars, the lid of which they used to rattle to attract notice and bring people to their doors.

[54] Hospital.

ORLANDO
I cannot abide, sir, to see a woman wronged, not I.

MATHEO
Sirrah, here was my father-in-law to day.

ORLANDO
Pish, then you're full of crowns.

MATHEO
Hang him! he would ha' thrust crowns upon me, to have fallen in again, but I scorn cast clothes, or any man's gold.

ORLANDO
But mine; [Aside.]—How did he brook that, sir?

MATHEO
Oh, swore like a dozen of drunken tinkers; at last growing foul in words, he and four of his men drew upon me, sir.

ORLANDO
In your house? would I had been by!

MATHEO
I made no more ado, but fell to my old lock, and so thrashed my blue-coats and old crab-tree-face my father-in-law, and then walked like a lion in my grate.

ORLANDO

O noble master!

MATHEO
Sirrah, he could tell me of the robbing the two pedlars, and that warrants are out for us both.

ORLANDO
Good sir, I like not those crackers.

MATHEO
Crackhalter, wou't set thy foot to mine?

ORLANDO
How, sir? at drinking.

MATHEO
We'll pull that old crow my father: rob thy master. I know the house, thou the servants: the purchase[55] is rich, the plot to get it is easy, the dog will not part from a bone.

[55] Booty.

ORLANDO
Pluck't out of his throat, then: I'll snarl for one, if this[289] can bite.

[289] Meaning his sword.

MATHEO
Say no more, say no more, old coal, meet me anon at the sign of the Shipwreck.

ORLANDO
Yes, sir.

MATHEO
And dost hear, man?—the Shipwreck.

[Exit.

ORLANDO
Th'art at the shipwreck now, and like a swimmer,
Bold, but inexpert, with those waves dost play,
Whose dalliance, whorelike, is to cast thee away.

Enter HIPPOLITO and BELLAFRONT.

And here's another vessel, better fraught,
But as ill-manned her sinking will be wrought,
If rescue come not: like a man of war
I'll therefore bravely out; somewhat I'll do,
And either save them both, or perish too.

[Exit.

HIPPOLITO
'Tis my fate to be bewitched by those eyes.

BELLAFRONT
Fate? your folly.
Why should my face thus mad you? 'Las, those colours
Are wound up long ago, which beauty spread;
The flowers that once grew here, are witherèd.
You turned my black soul white, made it look new,
And should I sin, it ne'er should be with you.

HIPPOLITO
Your hand, I'll offer you fair play: When first
We met i'th 'lists together, you remember
You were a common rebel; with one parley
I won you to come in.

BELLAFRONT
You did.

HIPPOLITO
I'll try
If now I can beat down this chastity
With the same ordnance; will you yield this fort,
If the power of argument now, as then,
I get of you the conquest: as before
I turned you honest, now to turn you whore,
By force of strong persuasion?

BELLAFRONT
If you can,
I yield.

HIPPOLITO
The alarum's struck up; I'm your man.

BELLAFRONT
A woman gives defiance.

HIPPOLITO
Sit.

[They seat themselves.

BELLAFRONT

Begin:
'Tis a brave battle to encounter sin.

HIPPOLITO
You men that are to fight in the same war
To which I'm prest, and plead at the same bar,
To win a woman, if you'd have me speed,
Send all your wishes!

BELLAFRONT
No doubt you're heard; proceed.

HIPPOLITO
To be a harlot, that you stand upon,
The very name's a charm to make you one.
Harlotta was a dame of so divine
And ravishing touch, that she was concubine
To an English king;[56] her sweet bewitching eye
Did the king's heart-strings in such love-knots tie,
That even the coyest was proud when she could hear
Men say, "behold, another harlot there!"
And after her all women that were fair
Were harlots called as to this day some are:
Besides, her dalliance she so well does mix,
That she's in Latin called the Meretrix.
Thus for the name; for the profession, this,
Who lives in bondage, lives laced; the chief bliss
This world below can yield, is liberty:
And who, than whores, with looser wings dare fly?
As Juno's proud bird spreads the fairest tail,
So does a strumpet hoist the loftiest sail,
She's no man's slave; men are her slaves; her eye
Moves not on wheels screwed up with jealousy.
She, horsed or coached, does merry journeys make,
Free as the sun in his gilt zodiac:
As bravely does she shine, as fast she's driven,
But stays not long in any house of heaven;
But shifts from sign to sign, her amorous prizes
More rich being when she's down, than when she rises.
In brief, gentlemen hunt them, soldiers fight for them,
Few men but know them, few or none abhor them:
Thus for sport's sake speak I, as to a woman,
Whom, as the worst ground, I would turn to common:
But you I would enclose for mine own bed.

[56] Steevens pointed out that Arlotte was not the concubine of an English king but was the mistress of the father of William the Conqueror.

BELLAFRONT
So should a husband be dishonourèd.

HIPPOLITO
Dishonoured? not a whit: to fall to one
Besides your husband is to fall to none,
For one no number is.

BELLAFRONT
Faith, should you take
One in your bed, would you that reckoning make?
'Tis time you found retreat.

HIPPOLITO
Say, have I won,
Is the day ours?

BELLAFRONT
The battle's but half done,
None but yourself have yet sounded alarms,
Let us strike too, else you dishonour arms.

HIPPOLITO
If you can win the day, the glory's yours.

BELLAFRONT
To prove a woman should not be a whore,
When she was made, she had one man, no more;
Yet she was tied to laws then, for even than,[57]
'Tis said, she was not made for men, but man.
Anon, t'increase earth's brood, the law was varied,
Men should take many wives: and though they married
According to that act, yet 'tis not known
But that those wives were only tied to one.
New parliaments were since: for now one woman
Is shared between three hundred, nay she's common,
Common as spotted leopards, whom for sport
Men hunt to get the flesh, but care not for't.
So spread they nets of gold, and tune their calls,
To enchant silly women to take falls;
Swearing they're angels, which that they may win
They'll hire the devil to come with false dice in.
Oh Sirens' subtle tunes! yourselves you flatter,
And our weak sex betray: so men love water;
It serves to wash their hands, but being once foul,
The water down is poured, cast out of doors,
And even of such base use do men make whores.
A harlot, like a hen more sweetness reaps,

To pick men one by one up, than in heaps:
Yet all feeds but confounding. Say you should taste me,
I serve but for the time, and when the day
Of war is done, am cashiered out of pay:
If like lame soldiers I could beg, that's all,
And there's lust's rendezvous, an hospital.
Who then would be a man's slave, a man's woman?
She's half starved the first day that feeds in common.

[57] i.e. Then.

HIPPOLITO
You should not feed so, but with me alone.

BELLAFRONT
If I drink poison by stealth, is't not all one?
Is't not rank poison still with you alone?
Nay, say you spied a courtesan, whose soft side
To touch you'd sell your birth-right, for one kiss
Be racked; she's won, you're sated: what follows this?
Oh, then you curse that bawd that tolled you in;
The night you curse your lust, you loathe the sin,
You loathe her very sight, and ere the day
Arise, you rise glad when you're stol'n away.
Even then when you are drunk with all her sweets,
There's no true pleasure in a strumpet's sheets.
Women whom lust so prostitutes to sale,
Like dancers upon ropes, once seen, are stale.

HIPPOLITO
If all the threads of harlot's lives are spun,
So coarse as you would make them, tell me why
You so long loved the trade?

BELLAFRONT
If all the threads
Of harlot's lives be fine as you would make them,
Why do not you persuade your wife turn whore,
And all dames else to fall before that sin?
Like an ill husband, though I knew the same
To be my undoing, followed I that game.
Oh, when the work of lust had earned my bread,
To taste it how I trembled, lest each bit,
Ere it went down, should choke me chewing it!
My bed seemed like a cabin hung in hell,
The bawd, hell's porter, and the liquorish wine
The pander fetched, was like an easy fine,
For which, methought, I leased away my soul,

And oftentimes, even in my quaffing bowl,
Thus said I to myself, I am a whore,
And have drunk down thus much confusion more.

HIPPOLITO
It is a common rule, and 'tis most true,
Two of one trade ne'er love: no more do you.
Why are you sharp 'gainst that you once professed?

BELLAFRONT
Why dote you on that, which you did once detest?
I cannot, seeing she's woven of such bad stuff,
Set colours on a harlot base enough.
Nothing did make me, when I loved them best,
To loathe them more than this: when in the street
A fair young modest damsel I did meet,
She seemed to all a dove, when I passed by,
And I to all a raven: every eye
That followed her went with a bashful glance,
At me each bold and jeering countenance
Darted forth scorn; to her as if she had been
Some tower unvanquished, would they vail,
'Gainst me swoln rumour hoisted every sail.
She, crowned with reverend praises, passed by them,
I, though with face masked, could not 'scape the hem,
For, as if Heaven had set strange marks on whores,
Because they should be pointing stocks to man,
Drest up in civilest shape, a courtesan—
Let her walk saint-like, noteless, and unknown,
Yet she's betrayed by some trick of her own.
Were harlots therefore wise, they'd be sold dear:
For men account them good but for one year,
And then like almanacs whose dates are gone,
They are thrown by, and no more looked upon.
Who'll therefore backward fall, who will launch forth
In seas so foul, for ventures no more worth?
Lust's voyage hath, if not this course, this cross,
Buy ne'er so cheap, your ware comes home with loss.
What, shall I sound retreat? the battle's done:
Let the world judge which of us two have won.

HIPPOLITO
I!

BELLAFRONT
You? nay then as cowards do in fight,
What by blows cannot, shall be saved by flight.

[Exit.

HIPPOLITO
Fly to earth's fixèd centre: to the caves
Of everlasting horror, I'll pursue thee,
Though loaden with sins, even to hell's brazen doors.
Thus wisest men turn fools, doting on whores.

[Exit.

SCENE II.—An Apartment in the Duke's Palace.

Enter the DUKE, LODOVICO, and ORLANDO, disguised as a SERVING-MAN; after them INFELICE, CAROLO, ASTOLFO, BERALDO, and FONTINELL.

ORLANDO
I beseech your grace, though your eye be so piercing as under a poor blue coat to cull out an honest father from an old serving-man, yet, good my lord, discover not the plot to any, but only this gentleman that is now to be an actor in our ensuing comedy.

DUKE
Thou hast thy wish, Orlando, pass unknown,
Sforza shall only go along with thee,
To see that warrant served upon thy son.

LODOVICO
To attach him upon felony, for two pedlars: is't not so?

ORLANDO
Right, my noble knight: those pedlars were two knaves of mine; he fleeced the men before, and now he purposes to flay the master. He will rob me; his teeth water to be nibbling at my gold, but this shall hang him by th' gills, till I pull him on shore.

DUKE
Away: ply you the business.

ORLANDO
Thanks to your grace: but, my good lord, for my daughter—

DUKE
You know what I have said.

ORLANDO
And remember what I have sworn. She's more honest, on my soul, than one of the Turks' wenches, watched by a hundred eunuchs.

LODOVICO

So she had need, for the Turks make them whores.

ORLANDO
He's a Turk that makes any woman a whore; he's no true
Christian, I'm sure. I commit your grace.

DUKE
Infelice.

INFELICE
Here, sir.

LODOVICO
Signor Friscobaldo.

ORLANDO
Frisking again? Pacheco.

LODOVICO
Uds so, Pacheco? we'll have some sport with this warrant: 'tis to apprehend all suspected persons in the house. Besides, there's one Bots a pander, and one Madam Horseleech a bawd, that have abused my friend; those two conies will we ferret into the purse-net.[58]

[58] A net, the mouth of which was drawn together with a string.

ORLANDO
Let me alone for dabbing them o'th' neck: come, come.

LODOVICO
Do ye hear, gallants? meet me anon at Matheo's.

CAROLO, ASTOLFO, &c. Enough.

[Exeunt LODOVICO and ORLANDO.

DUKE
Th' old fellow sings that note thou didst before
Only his tunes are, that she is no whore,
But that she sent his letters and his gifts,
Out of a noble triumph o'er his lust,
To show she trampled his assaults in dust.

INFELICE
'Tis a good honest servant, that old man.

DUKE
I doubt no less.

INFELICE
And it may be my husband,
Because when once this woman was unmasked,
He levelled all her thoughts, and made them fit,
Now he'd mar all again, to try his wit.

DUKE
It may be so too, for to turn a harlot
Honest, it must be by strong antidotes;
'Tis rare, as to see panthers change their spots.
And when she's once a star fixed and shines bright,
Though 'twere impiety then to dim her light,
Because we see such tapers seldom burn,
Yet 'tis the pride and glory of some men,
To change her to a blazing star again,
And it may be, Hippolito does no more.
It cannot be but you're acquainted all
With that same madness of our son-in law,
That dotes so on a courtesan.

ALL
Yes, my lord.

CAROLO
All the city thinks he's a whoremonger.

ASTOLFO
Yet I warrant he'll swear no man marks him.

BERALDO
'Tis like so, for when a man goes a wenching, it is as if he had a strong stinking breath, every one smells him out, yet he feels it not, though it be ranker than the sweat of sixteen bear warders.

DUKE
I doubt then you have all those stinking breaths, You might be all smelt out.

CAROLO
Troth, my lord, I think we are all as you ha' been in your youth when you went a-maying, we all love to hear the cuckoo sing upon other men's trees.

DUKE
It's well; yet you confess. But, girl, thy bed
Shall not be parted with a courtesan.
'Tis strange,
No frown of mine, no frown of the poor lady,
My abused child, his wife, no care of fame,
Of honour, heaven, or hell, no not that name
Of common strumpet, can affright, or woo him

To abandon her; the harlot does undo him;
She has bewitched him, robbed him of his shape,
Turned him into a beast, his reason's lost;
You see he looks wild, does he not?

CAROLO
I ha' noted new moons
In's face, my lord, all full of change.

DUKE
He's no more like unto Hippolito,
Than dead men are to living—never sleeps,
Or if he do, it's dreams: and in those dreams
His arms work, and then cries, Sweet—what's her name,
What's the drab's name?

ASTOLFO
In troth, my lord, I know not,
I know no drabs, not I.

DUKE
Oh, Bellafront!—
And, catching her fast, cries, My Bellafront!

CAROLO
A drench that's able to kill a horse, cannot kill this disease of smock smelling, my lord, if it have once eaten deep.

DUKE
I'll try all physic, and this medicine first:
I have directed warrants strong and peremptory
To purge our city Milan, and to cure
The outward parts, the suburbs, for the attaching
Of all those women, who like gold want weight,
Cities, like ships, should have no idle freight.

CAROLO
No, my lord, and light wenches are no idle freight; but what's your grace's reach in this?

DUKE
This, Carolo. If she whom my son doats on,
Be in that muster-book enrolled, he'll shame
Ever t'approach one of such noted name.

CAROLO
But say she be not?

DUKE

Yet on harlots' heads
New laws shall fall so heavy, and such blows shall
Give to those that haunt them, that Hippolito
If not for fear of law, for love to her,
If he love truly, shall her bed forbear.

CAROLO
Attach all the light heels i'th' city, and clap 'em up? Why, my lord, you dive into a well unsearchable: all the whores within the walls, and without the walls? I would not be he should meddle with them for ten such dukedoms; the army that you speak on is able to fill all the prisons within this city, and to leave not a drinking room in any tavern besides.

DUKE
Those only shall be caught that are of note;
Harlots in each street flow:
The fish being thus i'th net, ourself will sit,
And with eye most severe dispose of it.
Come, girl.

[Exeunt DUKE and INFELICE.

CAROLO
Arraign the poor whores!

ASTOLFO
I'll not miss that sessions.

Font. Nor I.

BERALDO
Nor I, though I hold up my hand there myself.

[Exeunt.

SCENE III.—A Room in Matheo's House.

Enter MATHEO, LODOVICO, and ORLANDO disguised as a SERVING-MAN.

MATHEO
Let who will come, my noble chevalier, I can but play the kind host, and bid 'em welcome.

LODOVICO
We'll trouble your house, Matheo, but as Dutchmen do in taverns, drink, be merry, and be gone.

ORLANDO
Indeed, if you be right Dutchmen, if you fall to drinking, you must be gone.

MATHEO
The worst is, my wife is not at home; but we'll fly high, my generous knight, for all that: there's no music when a woman is in the concert.

ORLANDO
No; for she's like a pair of virginals,
Always with jacks at her tail.

Enter ASTOLFO, CAROLO, BERALDO and FONTINELL.

LODOVICO
See, the covey is sprung.

ASTOLFO, CAROLO, &c.
Save you, gallants.

MATHEO
Happily encountered, sweet bloods.

LODOVICO
Gentlemen, you all know Signor Candido, the linen-draper, he that's more patient than a brown baker, upon the day when he heats his oven, and has forty scolds about him.

ASTOLFO, CAROLO, &c.
Yes, we know him all, what of him?

LODOVICO
Would it not be a good fit of mirth, to make a piece of English cloth of him, and to stretch him on the tenters, till the threads of his own natural humour crack, by making him drink healths, tobacco,[59] dance, sing bawdy songs, or to run any bias according as we think good to cast him?

[59] To drink tobacco was a common phrase for smoking it.—Reed.

CAROLO
'Twere a morris-dance worth the seeing.

ASTOLFO
But the old fox is so crafty, we shall hardly hunt him out of his den.

MATHEO
To that train I ha' given fire already; and the hook to draw him hither, is to see certain pieces of lawn, which I told him I have to sell, and indeed have such; fetch them down, Pacheco.

ORLANDO
Yes, sir, I'm your water-spaniel, and will fetch any thing—but I'll fetch one dish of meat anon shall turn your stomach, and that's a constable.

[Aside and exit.

Enter BOTS ushering in Mistress HORSELEECH.

ASTOLFO, BERALDO, FONTINELL
How now? how now?

CAROLO
What gally-foist[60] is this?

[60] A long barge with oars.

LODOVICO
Peace, two dishes of stewed prunes,[61] a bawd and a pander. My worthy lieutenant Bots; why, now I see thou'rt a man of thy word, welcome.—Welcome Mistress Horseleech: pray, gentlemen, salute this reverend matron.

[61] A common dish in the brothels of the time.

Mistress HORSELEECH
Thanks to all your worships.

LODOVICO
I bade a drawer send in wine, too: did none come along with thee, grannam, but the lieutenant?

Mistress HORSELEECH
None came along with me but Bots, if it like your worship.

BOTS
Who the pox should come along with you but Bots.

Enter two VINTERS with wine.

ASTOLFO, CAROLO, &c.
Oh brave! march fair.

LODOVICO
Are you come? that's well.

MATHEO
Here's ordnance able to sack a city.

LODOVICO
Come, repeat, read this inventory.

1st VINTER
Imprimis, a pottle of Greek wine, a pottle of Peter-sameene,[62] a pottle of Charnico,[63] and a pottle of Leatica.[64]

[62] *A corruption of Pedro Ximenes, a sweet Spanish wine, so called from the grape of that name.*

[63] *A sweet Portuguese wine from the neighbourhood of Lisbon.*

[64] *i.e. Aleatico, a red Italian muscatel wine with a rich aromatic flavour.*

LODOVICO
You're paid?

2nd VINTER
Yes, Sir.

[Exeunt VINTERS.

MATHEO
So shall some of us be anon, I fear.

BOTS
Here's a hot day towards: but zounds, this is the life out of which a soldier sucks sweetness! when this artillery goes off roundly, some must drop to the ground: cannon, demi-cannon, saker, and basilisk.[65]

[65] *The saker and basilisk were both pieces of ordnance.*

LODOVICO
Give fire, lieutenant.

BOTS
So, so: Must I venture first upon the breach? to you all, gallants: Bots sets upon you all.

[Drinks.

ASTOLFO, CAROLO, &c.
It's hard, Bots, if we pepper not you, as well as you pepper us.

Enter CANDIDO.

LODOVICO
My noble linen-draper!—some wine!—Welcome old lad!

MATHEO
You're welcome, signor.

CANDIDO
These lawns, sir?

MATHEO
Presently; my man is gone for them: we ha' rigged a fleet, you see here, to sail about the world.

CANDIDO
A dangerous voyage, sailing in such ships.

BOTS
There's no casting over board yet.

LODOVICO
Because you are an old lady, I will have you be acquainted with this grave citizen, pray bestow your lips upon him, and bid him welcome.

Mistress HORSELEECH
Any citizen shall be most welcome to me:—I have used to buy ware at your shop.

CANDIDO
It may be so, good madam.

Mistress HORSELEECH
Your prentices know my dealings well; I trust your good wife be in good case: if it please you, bear her a token from my lips, by word of mouth.

[Kisses him.

CANDIDO
I pray no more; forsooth, 'tis very well,
Indeed I love no sweetmeats:—Sh'as a breath
Stinks worse than fifty polecats. [Aside.] Sir, a word,
Is she a lady?

LODOVICO
A woman of a good house, and an ancient, she's a bawd.

CANDIDO
A bawd? Sir, I'll steal hence, and see your lawns
Some other time.

MATHEO
Steal out of such company? Pacheco, my man is but gone for 'em: Lieutenant Bots, drink to this worthy old fellow, and teach him to fly high.

LODOVICO, ASTOLFO, &c.
Swagger: and make him do't on his knees.

CANDIDO
How, Bots? now bless me, what do I with Bots?
No wine in sooth, no wine, good Master Bots.

BOTS

Gray-beard, goat's pizzle: 'tis a health, have this in your guts, or this, there [Touching his sword.] I will sing a bawdy song, sir, because your verjuice face is melancholy, to make liquor go down glib. Will you fall on your marrowbones, and pledge this health? 'Tis to my mistress, a whore.

CANDIDO
Here's ratsbane upon ratsbane, Master Bots;
I pray, sir, pardon me: you are a soldier,
Press me not to this service, I am old,
And shoot not in such pot-guns.[66]

[66] A play upon "pop-guns."

BOTS
Cap. I'll teach you.

CANDIDO
To drink healths, is to drink sickness—gentlemen.
Pray rescue me.

BOTS
Zounds, who dare?

LODOVICO, ASTOLFO, &c.
We shall ha' stabbing then?

CANDIDO
I ha' reckonings to cast up, good Master Bots.

BOTS
This will make you cast 'em up better.

LODOVICO
Why does your hand shake so?

CANDIDO
The palsy, signor, danceth in my blood.

BOTS
Pipe with a pox, sir, then, or I'll make your blood dance—

CANDIDO
Hold, hold, good Master Bots, I drink. [Kneels.[67]

[67] It was a common custom to kneel when drinking a health, especially the health of a superior.

ASTOLFO, LODOVICO, &c.
To whom?

CANDIDO
To the old countess there. [Drinks.

Mistress HORSELEECH
To me, old boy? this is he that never drunk wine!
Once again to't.

CANDIDO
With much ado the poison is got down,
Though I can scarce get up; never before
Drank I a whore's health, nor will never more.

Re-enter ORLANDO with lawns.

MATHEO
Hast been at gallows?

ORLANDO
Yes, sir, for I make account to suffer to day.

MATHEO
Look, signor; here's the commodity.

CANDIDO
Your price?

MATHEO
Thus.[68]

[68] The price was here probably indicated by displaying the fingers.

CANDIDO
No: too dear: thus.

MATHEO
No: O fie, you must fly higher: yet take 'em home, trifles shall not make us quarrel, we'll agree, you shall have them, and a pennyworth; I'll fetch money at your shop.

CANDIDO
Be it so, good signor, send me going.

MATHEO
Going? a deep bowl of wine for Signor Candido.

ORLANDO
He would be going.

CANDIDO

I'll rather stay than go so: stop your bowl.

Enter CONSTABLE and BILLMEN.

LODOVICO
How now?

BOTS
Is't Shrove-Tuesday, that these ghosts walk?[69]

[69] *On Shrove Tuesday the authorities made a search for brothel-keepers, and on the same day the London apprentices went about wrecking houses of ill-fame.*

MATHEO
What's your business, sir?

CONSTABLE
From the duke: you are the man we look for, signor. I have warrant here from the duke, to apprehend you upon felony for robbing two pedlars: I charge you i'th' duke's name go quickly.

MATHEO
Is the wind turned? Well: this is that old wolf, my father-in-law:—seek out your mistress, sirrah.

ORLANDO
Yes, Sir,—as shafts by piecing are made strong,
So shall thy life be straightened by this wrong.

[Aside and exit.

LODOVICO, ASTOLFO, &c.
In troth, we are sorry.

MATHEO
Brave men must be crossed; pish, it's but fortune's dice roving against me. Come, sir, pray use me like a gentleman; let me not be carried through the streets like a pageant.

CONSTABLE
If these gentlemen please, you shall go along with them.

LODOVICO, ASTOLFO, &c.
Be't so: come.

CONSTABLE
What are you, sir?

BOTS
I, sir? sometimes a figure, sometimes a cipher, as the
State has occasion to cast up her accounts: I'm a soldier.

CONSTABLE
Your name is Bots, is't not?

BOTS
Bots is my name; Bots is known to this company.

CONSTABLE
I know you are, sir: what's she?

BOTS
A gentlewoman, my mother.

CONSTABLE
Take 'em both along.

BOTS
Me, sir?

BILLMEN
Ay, sir!

CONSTABLE
If he swagger, raise the street.

BOTS
Gentlemen, gentlemen, whither will you drag us?

LODOVICO
To the garden house. Bots, are we even with you?

CONSTABLE
To Bridewell with 'em.

BOTS
You will answer this.

CONSTABLE
Better than a challenge. I've warrant for my work, sir.

LODOVICO
We'll go before.

CONSTABLE
Pray do.—

[Exeunt MATHEO with LODOVICO, ASTOLFO, CAROLO, BERALDO, and FONTINELL; BOTS and Mistress HORSELEECH, with BILLMEN.

Who, Signor Candido? a citizen
Of your degree consorted thus, and revelling
In such a house?

CANDIDO
Why, sir? what house, I pray?

CONSTABLE
Lewd, and defamed.

CANDIDO
Is't so? thanks, sir: I'm gone.

CONSTABLE
What have you there?

CANDIDO
Lawns which I bought, sir, of the gentleman that keeps the house.

CONSTABLE
And I have warrant here,
To search for such stol'n ware: these lawns are stol'n.

CANDIDO
Indeed!

CONSTABLE
So he's the thief, you the receiver:
I'm sorry for this chance, I must commit you.

CANDIDO
Me, sir, for what?

CONSTABLE
These goods are found upon you,
And you must answer't.

CANDIDO
Must I so?

CONSTABLE
Most certain.

CANDIDO
I'll send for bail.

CONSTABLE

I dare not: yet because
You are a citizen of worth, you shall not
Be made a pointing stock, but without guard,
Pass only with myself.

CANDIDO
To Bridewell too?

CONSTABLE
No remedy.

CANDIDO
Yes, patience: being not mad,
They had me once to Bedlam, now I'm drawn
To Bridewell, loving no whores.

CONSTABLE
You will buy lawn!

[Exeunt.

ACT THE FIFTH.

SCENE I.—A Street.

Enter at one side HIPPOLITO; at the other, LODOVICO, ASTOLFO, CAROLO, BERALDO and FONTINELL.

LODOVICO
Yonder's the Lord Hippolito; by any means leave him and me together; now will I turn him to a madman.

ASTOLFO, CAROLO, &c
Save you my lord.

[Exeunt all except HIPPOLITO and LODOVICO.

LODOVICO
I ha' strange news to tell you.

HIPPOLITO
What are they?

LODOVICO
Your mare's i'th' pound.

HIPPOLITO
How's this?

LODOVICO
Your nightingale is in a limebush.

HIPPOLITO
Ha?

LODOVICO
Your puritanical honest whore sits in a blue gown.[69]

[69] It was in a blue gown that strumpets had to do penance.

HIPPOLITO
Blue gown!

LODOVICO
She'll chalk out your way to her now: she beats chalk.

HIPPOLITO
Where? who dares?—

LODOVICO
Do you know the brick-house of castigation, by the river side[70] that runs by Milan,—the school where they pronounce no letter well but O?

[70] Meaning Bridewell, where loose women were whipped.

HIPPOLITO
I know it not.

LODOVICO
Any man that has borne office of constable, or any woman that has fallen from a horse-load to a cart-load,[71] or like an old hen that has had none but rotten eggs in her nest, can direct you to her: there you shall see your punk amongst her back-friends.

[71] An allusion to the carting of prostitutes, who were at the same time pelted by the populace with rotten eggs.

There you may have her at your will,
For there she beats chalk, or grinds in the mill[72]
With a whip deedle, deedle, deedle, deedle;
Ah little monkey.

[72] Breaking chalk, grinding in mills, raising sand and gravel and making of lime were among the employments assigned to vagrants and others committed to Bridewell.—Reed.

HIPPOLITO
What rogue durst serve that warrant, knowing I loved her?

LODOVICO
Some worshipful rascal, I lay my life.

HIPPOLITO
I'll beat the lodgings down about their ears
That are her keepers.

LODOVICO
So you may bring an old house over her head.

HIPPOLITO
I'll to her—
I'll to her, stood armed fiends to guard the doors.

[Exit.

LODOVICO
Oh me! what monsters are men made by whores!
If this false fire do kindle him, there's one faggot
More to the bonfire. Now to my Bridewell birds;
What song will they sing?

[Exit.

SCENE II.—An Apartment in Bridewell.

Enter DUKE, INFELICE, CAROLO, ASTOLFO, BERALDO, FONTINELL, and several MASTERS of Bridewell.

DUKE
Your Bridewell? that the name? for beauty, strength,
Capacity and form of ancient building,
Besides the river's neighbourhood, few houses
Wherein we keep our court can better it.

1st MASTER
Hither from foreign courts have princes come,
And with our duke did acts of State commence,
Here that great cardinal had first audience,
The grave Campayne; that duke dead, his son
That famous prince gave free possession
Of this, his palace, to the citizens,
To be the poor man's ware-house; and endowed it
With lands to the value of seven hundred marks,[73]
With all the bedding and the furniture, once proper,
As the lands then were, to an hospital

Belonging to a Duke of Savoy. Thus
Fortune can toss the world; a prince's court
Is thus a prison now.

[73] *This and the subsequent allusions to the Bridewell of* Milan, of course, really have reference to the London Bridewell. In the reign of Henry VIII. princes were lodged there, and it was there that Cardinal Campeius had his first audience of the king. After Henry's death, Edward VI. gave the palace to the citizens. It was moreover endowed with land belonging to the Savoy to the amount of 700 marks a year and the bedding and furniture of this hospital were bestowed upon it.

DUKE
'Tis Fortune's sport:
These changes common are: the wheel of fate
Turns kingdoms up, till they fall desolate.
But how are these seven hundred marks by th' year
Employed in this your work-house?

1st MASTER
War and peace
Feed both upon those lands: when the iron doors
Of war burst open, from this house are sent
Men furnished in all martial complement.
The moon hath thorough her bow scarce drawn to th' head,
Like to twelve silver arrows, all the months,
Since sixteen hundred soldiers went abroad.
Here providence and charity play such parts,
The house is like a very school of arts,
For when our soldiers, like ships driven from sea,
With ribs all broken, and with tattered sides,
Cast anchor here again, their ragged backs
How often do we cover! that, like men,
They may be sent to their own homes again.
All here are but one swarm of bees, and strive
To bring with wearied thighs honey to the hive.
The sturdy beggar, and the lazy loon,
Gets here hard hands, or laced correction.
The vagabond grows staid, and learns t'obey,
The drone is beaten well, and sent away.
As other prisons are, some for the thief,
Some, by which undone credit gets relief
From bridled debtors; others for the poor,
So this is for the bawd, the rogue, the whore.

CAROLO
An excellent team of horse!

1st MASTER
Nor is it seen

That the whip draws blood here, to cool the spleen
Of any rugged bencher; nor does offence
Feel smart on spiteful, or rash evidence:
But pregnant testimony forth must stand,
Ere justice leave them in the beadle's hand,
As iron, on the anvil are they laid,
Not to take blows alone, but to be made
And fashioned to some charitable use.

DUKE
Thus wholsom'st laws spring from the worst abuse.

Enter ORLANDO, disguised as a SERVING-MAN, and BELLAFRONT.

BELLAFRONT
Let mercy touch your heart-strings, gracious lord,
That it may sound like music in the ear
Of a man desperate, being i'th' hands of law.

DUKE
His name?

BELLAFRONT
Matheo.

DUKE
For a robbery? Where is he?

BELLAFRONT
In this house.

[Exeunt BELLAFRONT and 2nd MASTER.

DUKE
Fetch you him hither—Is this the party?

ORLANDO
This is the hen, my lord, that the cock with the lordly comb, your son-in-law, would crow over, and tread.

DUKE
Are your two servants ready?

ORLANDO
My two pedlars are packed together, my good lord.

DUKE
'Tis well: this day in judgment shall be spent:

Vice, like a wound lanced, mends by punishment.

INFELICE
Let me be gone, my lord, or stand unseen;
'Tis rare when a judge strikes, and that none die,
And 'tis unfit then women should be by.

1st MASTER
We'll place you, lady, in some private room.

INFELICE
Pray do so.

[Exit with 1st MASTER, who returns alone.

ORLANDO
Thus nice dames swear, it is unfit their eyes
Should view men carved up for anatomies,[74]
Yet they'll see all, so they may stand unseen;
Many women sure will sin behind a screen.

[74] i.e. Skeletons.

Enter LODOVICO.

LODOVICO
Your son, the Lord Hippolito, is entered.

DUKE
Tell him we wish his presence. A word, Sforza;
On what wings flew he hither?

LODOVICO
These—I told him his lark whom he loved, was a Bridewell-bird; he's mad that this cage should hold her, and is come to let her out.

DUKE
'Tis excellent: away, go call him hither.

[Exit LODOVICO.

Re-enter on one side 2nd MASTER and BELLAFRONT with MATHEO, and CONSTABLE; on the other, LODOVICO with HIPPOLITO. ORLANDO goes out, and returns with two of his SERVANTS disguised as PEDLARS.

DUKE
You are to us a stranger, worthy lord,
'Tis strange to see you here.

HIPPOLITO
It is most fit,
That where the sun goes, atomies[75] follow it.

[75] Atoms.

DUKE
Atomies neither shape, nor honour bear:
Be you yourself, a sunbeam to shine clear.—
Is this the gentleman? Stand forth and hear
Your accusation.

MATHEO
I'll hear none: I fly high in that: rather than kites shall seize upon me, and pick out mine eyes to my face, I'll strike my talons through mine own heart first, and spit my blood in theirs. I am here for shriving those two fools of their sinful pack: when those jackdaws have cawed over me, then must I cry guilty, or not guilty; the law has work enough already and therefore I'll put no work of mine into his hands; the hangman shall ha't first; I did pluck those ganders, did rob them.

DUKE
'Tis well done to confess.

MATHEO
Confess and be hanged, and then I fly high, is't not so? That for that; a gallows is the worst rub that a good bowler can meet with; I stumbled against such a post, else this night I had played the part of a true son in these days, undone my father-in-law; with him would I ha' run at leap-frog, and come over his gold, though I had broke his neck for't: but the poor salmon-trout is now in the net.

HIPPOLITO
And now the law must teach you to fly high.

MATHEO
Right, my lord, and then may you fly low; no more words:—a mouse, mum, you are stopped.

BELLAFRONT
Be good to my poor husband, dear my lords.

MATHEO
Ass!
Why shouldst thou pray them to be good to me,
When no man here is good to one another?

DUKE
Did any hand work in this theft but yours?

MATHEO

O, yes, my lord, yes:—the hangman has never one son at a birth, his children always come by couples: though I cannot give the old dog, my father, a bone to gnaw, the daughter shall be sure of a choke-pear.[76] Yes, my lord, there was one more that fiddled my fine pedlars, and that was my wife.

[76] Slang term for a small copper coin.

BELLAFRONT
Alas, I?

ORLANDO
O everlasting, supernatural superlative villain! [Aside.

DUKE, LODOVICO, &c
Your wife, Matheo?

HIPPOLITO
Sure it cannot be.

MATHEO
Oh, sir, you love no quarters of mutton that hang up, you love none but whole mutton. She set the robbery, I performed it; she spurred me on, I galloped away.

ORLANDO
My lords,—

BELLAFRONT
My lords,—fellow, give me speech,—if my poor life
May ransom thine, I yield it to the law,
Thou hurt'st thy soul, yet wip'st off no offence,
By casting blots upon my innocence:
Let not these spare me, but tell truth: no, see
Who slips his neck out of the misery,
Though not out of the mischief: let thy servant
That shared in this base act, accuse me here,
Why should my husband perish, he go clear?

ORLANDO
A good child, hang thine own father! [Aside.

DUKE
Old fellow, was thy hand in too?

ORLANDO
My hand was in the pie, my lord, I confess it: my mistress, I see, will bring me to the gallows, and so leave me; but I'll not leave her so: I had rather hang in a woman's company, than in a man's; because if we should go to hell together, I should scarce be letten in, for all the devils are afraid to have any women come amongst them. As I am true thief, she neither consented to this felony, nor knew of it.

DUKE
What fury prompts thee on to kill thy wife?

MATHEO
It is my humour, sir, 'tis a foolish bag-pipe that I make myself merry with: why should I eat hemp-seed at the hangman's thirteen-pence halfpenny[77] ordinary, and have this whore laugh at me, as I swing, as I totter?

[77] *The amount of the hangman's fee.*

DUKE
Is she a whore?

MATHEO
A six-penny mutton pasty, for any to cut up.

ORLANDO
Ah, toad, toad, toad.

MATHEO
A barber's cittern[78] for every serving-man to play upon; that lord, your son, knows it.

[78] *A cittern or lute was part of the appointments of a barber's shop of the period.*

HIPPOLITO
I, sir? Am I her bawd then?

MATHEO
No, sir, but she's your whore then.

ORLANDO
Yea, spider; dost catch at great flies? [Aside.

HIPPOLITO
My whore?

MATHEO
I cannot talk, sir, and tell of your rems and your rees and your whirligigs and devices: but, my lord, I found 'em like sparrows in one nest, billing together, and bulling of me. I took 'em in bed, was ready to kill him, was up to stab her—

HIPPOLITO
Close thy rank jaws:—pardon me, I am vexed;
Thou art a villain, a malicious devil,
Deep as the place where thou art lost, thou liest,
Since I am thus far got into this storm,
I'll through, and thou shall see I'll through untouched,
When thou shalt perish in it.

Re-enter INFELICE.

INFELICE
'Tis my cue,
To enter now.—Room! let my prize be played;
I ha' lurked in clouds, yet heard what all have said;
What jury more can prove sh'as wronged my bed,
Than her own husband; she must be punishèd.
I challenge law, my lord; letters and gold,
And jewels from my lord that woman took.

HIPPOLITO
Against that black-mouthed devil, against letters and gold,
And against a jealous wife, I do uphold
Thus far her reputation; I could sooner
Shake th' Appenine, and crumble rocks to dust,
Than, though Jove's shower rained down, tempt her to lust.

BELLAFRONT
What shall I say?

ORLANDO
[Throwing off his disguise.] Say thou art not a whore, and that's more than fifteen women amongst five hundred dare swear without lying: this shalt thou say—no, let me say't for thee—thy husband's a knave, this lord's an honest man; thou art no punk, this lady's a right lady. Pacheco is a thief as his master is, but old Orlando is as true a man as thy father is. I ha' seen you fly high, sir, and I ha' seen you fly low, sir, and to keep you from the gallows, sir, a blue coat have I worn, and a thief did I turn. Mine own men are the pedlars, my twenty pounds did fly high, sir, your wife's gown did fly low, sir: whither fly you now, sir? you ha' scaped the gallows, to the devil you fly next, sir. Am I right, my liege?

DUKE
Your father has the true physician played.

MATHEO
And I am now his patient.

HIPPOLITO
And be so still;
'Tis a good sign when our cheeks blush at ill.

CONSTABLE
The linen-draper, Signor Candido,
He whom the city terms the patient man,
Is likewise here for buying of those lawns
The pedlars lost.

INFELICE

Alas, good Candido!

DUKE
Fetch him

[Exit CONSTABLE]

—and when these payments up are cast,
Weigh out your light gold, but let's have them last.

Enter CANDIDO and CONSTABLE, who presently goes out.

DUKE
In Bridewell, Candido?

CANDIDO
Yes, my good lord.

DUKE
What make you here?

CANDIDO
My lord, what make you here?

DUKE
I'm here to save right, and to drive wrong hence.

CANDIDO
And I to bear wrong here with patience.

DUKE
You ha' bought stol'n goods.

CANDIDO
So they do say, my lord,
Yet bought I them upon a gentleman's word,
And I imagine now, as I thought then,
That there be thieves, but no thieves, gentlemen.

HIPPOLITO
Your credit's cracked, being here.

CANDIDO
No more than gold
Being cracked, which does his estimation hold.
I was in Bedlam once, but was I mad?
They made me pledge whores' healths, but am I bad
Because I'm with bad people?

DUKE
Well, stand by;
If you take wrong, we'll cure the injury.

Re-enter CONSTABLE, after him BOTS, then two BEADLES, one with hemp, the other with a beetle.[79]

[79] A heavy mallet.

DUKE
Stay, stay, what's he? a prisoner?

CONSTABLE
Yes, my lord.

HIPPOLITO
He seems a soldier?

BOTS
I am what I seem, sir, one of fortune's bastards, a soldier and a gentleman, and am brought in here with master constable's band of billmen, because they face me down that I live, like those that keep bowling alleys, by the sins of the people, in being a squire of the body.

HIPPOLITO
Oh, an apple-squire.[80]

[80] The term was applied both to a kept gallant and to a pander.

BOTS
Yes, sir, that degree of scurvy squires; and that I am maintained by the best part that is commonly in a woman, by the worst players of those parts; but I am known to all this company.

LODOVICO
My lord, 'tis true, we all know him, 'tis Lieutenant Bots.

DUKE
Bots, and where ha' you served, Bots?

BOTS
In most of your hottest services in the Low-countries: at the Groyne I was wounded in this thigh, and halted upon't, but 'tis now sound. In Cleveland I missed but little, having the bridge of my nose broken down with two great stones, as I was scaling a fort. I ha' been tried, sir, too, in Gelderland, and 'scaped hardly there from being blown up at a breach: I was fired, and lay i' th' surgeon's hands for't, till the fall of the leaf following.

HIPPOLITO
All this may be, and yet you no soldier.

BOTS
No soldier, sir? I hope these are services that your proudest commanders do venture upon, and never come off sometimes.

DUKE
Well, sir, because you say you are a soldier,
I'll use you like a gentleman.—Make room there,
Plant him amongst you; we shall have anon
Strange hawks fly here before us: if none light
On you, you shall with freedom take your flight:
But if you prove a bird of baser wing,
We'll use you like such birds, here you shall sing.

BOTS
I wish to be tried at no other weapon.

DUKE
Why, is he furnished with those implements?

1st MASTER
The pander is more dangerous to a State,
Than is the common thief; and though our laws
Lie heavier on the thief, yet that the pander
May know the hangman's ruff should fit him too,
Therefore he's set to beat hemp.

DUKE
This does savour
Of justice; basest slaves to basest labour.
Now pray, set open hell, and let us see
The she-devils that are here.

INFELICE
Methinks this place
Should make e'en Lais honest.

1st MASTER
Some it turns good,
But as some men, whose hands are once in blood,
Do in a pride spill more, so, some going hence,
Are, by being here, lost in more impudence.
Let it not to them, when they come, appear
That any one does as their judge sit here:
But that as gentlemen you come to see,
And then perhaps their tongues will walk more free.

DUKE
Let them be marshalled in.—

[Exeunt 1st and 2nd MASTERS, CONSTABLE, and BEADLES.]

—Be covered all,
Fellows, now to make the scene more comical.

CAROLO
Will not you be smelt out, Bots?

BOTS
No, your bravest whores have the worse noses.

Re-enter 1st and 2nd MASTERS and CONSTABLE, then DOROTHEA TARGET, brave[81]; after her two BEADLES, the one with a wheel, the other with a blue gown.

[81] Smartly attired.

LODOVICO
Are not you a bride, forsooth?

DOROTHEA TARGET
Say ye?

CAROLO
He would know if these be not your bridemen.

DOROTHEA TARGET
Vuh! yes, sir: and look ye, do you see? the bride-laces that I give at my wedding, will serve to tie rosemary to both your coffins when you come from hanging—Scab!

ORLANDO
Fie, punk, fie, fie, fie!

DOROTHEA TARGET
Out, you stale, stinking head of garlic, foh, at my heels.

ORLANDO
My head's cloven.

HIPPOLITO
O, let the gentlewoman alone, she's going to shrift.

ASTOLFO
Nay, to do penance.

CAROLO
Ay, ay, go, punk, go to the cross and be whipt.

DOROTHEA TARGET
Marry mew, marry muff,[82] marry, hang you, goodman dog: whipt? do ye take me for a base spittle-whore? In troth, gentlemen, you wear the clothes of gentlemen, but you carry not the minds of gentlemen, to abuse a gentlewoman of my fashion.

[82] A term of contempt.

LODOVICO
Fashion? pox a' your fashions! art not a whore?

DOROTHEA TARGET
Goodman slave.

DUKE
O fie, abuse her not, let us two talk,
What might I call your name, pray?

DOROTHEA TARGET
I'm not ashamed of my name, sir; my name is Mistress Doll Target, a Western gentlewoman.

LODOVICO
Her target against any pike in Milan.

DUKE
Why is this wheel borne after her?

1st MASTER
She must spin.

DOROTHEA TARGET
A coarse thread it shall be, as all threads are.

ASTOLFO
If you spin, then you'll earn money here too?

DOROTHEA TARGET
I had rather get half-a-crown abroad, than ten crowns here.

ORLANDO
Abroad? I think so.

INFELICE
Dost thou not weep now thou art here?

DOROTHEA TARGET
Say ye? weep? yes, forsooth, as you did when you lost your maidenhead: do you not hear how I weep? [Sings.

LODOVICO
Farewell, Doll.

DOROTHEA TARGET
Farewell, dog.

[Exit.

DUKE
Past shame: past penitence! Why is that blue gown?

1st MASTER
Being stript out of her wanton loose attire,
That garment she puts on, base to the eye,
Only to clothe her in humility.

DUKE
Are all the rest like this?

1st MASTER
No, my good lord.
You see, this drab swells with a wanton rein,
The next that enters has a different strain.

DUKE
Variety is good, let's see the rest.

[Exeunt 1st and 2nd MASTERS and CONSTABLE.

BOTS
Your grace sees I'm sound yet, and no bullets hit me.

DUKE
Come off so, and 'tis well.

LODOVICO, ASTOLFO, &c. Here's the second mess.

Re-enter 1st and 2nd MASTERS and CONSTABLE, then PENELOPE WHOREHOUND, dressed like a Citizen's Wife; her two BEADLES, one with a blue gown, another with chalk and a mallet.

PENELOPE
I ha' worn many a costly gown, but I was never thus guarded[83] with blue coats, and beadles, and constables, and—

[83] A play upon the word, which also signifies "trimmed."

CAROLO

Alas, fair mistress, spoil not thus your eyes.

PENELOPE
Oh, sweet sir, I fear the spoiling of other places about me that are dearer than my eyes; if you be gentlemen, if you be men, or ever came of a woman, pity my case! stand to me, stick to me, good sir, you are an old man.

ORLANDO
Hang not on me, I prithee, old trees bear no such fruit.

PENELOPE
Will you bail me, gentlemen?

LODOVICO
Bail thee? art in for debt?

PENELOPE
No; God is my judge, sir, I am in for no debts; I paid my tailor for this gown, the last five shillings a-week that was behind, yesterday.

DUKE
What is your name, I pray?

PENELOPE
Penelope Whorehound, I come of the Whorehounds. How does Lieutenant Bots?

LODOVICO, ASTOLFO, &c
Aha, Bots!

BOTS
A very honest woman, as I'm a soldier—a pox Bots ye.

PENELOPE
I was never in this pickle before; and yet if I go amongst citizens' wives, they jeer at me; if I go among the loose-bodied gowns,[84] they cry a pox on me, because I go civilly attired, and swear their trade was a good trade, till such as I am took it out of their hands. Good Lieutenant Bots, speak to these captains to bail me.

[84] Prostitutes.

1st MASTER
Begging for bail still? you are a trim gossip;
Go give her the blue gown, set her to her chare.[85]
Work huswife, for your bread, away.

[85] Task work.

PENELOPE

Out, you dog!—a pox on you all!—women are born to curse thee—but I shall live to see twenty such flat-caps shaking dice for a penny-worth of pippins—out, you blue-eyed rogue. [Exit.

LODOVICO, ASTOLFO, &c.
Ha, ha, ha.

DUKE
Even now she wept, and prayed; now does she curse?

1st MASTER
Seeing me; if still sh' had stayed, this had been worse.

HIPPOLITO
Was she ever here before?

1st MASTER
Five times at least,
And thus if men come to her, have her eyes
Wrung, and wept out her bail.

LODOVICO, ASTOLFO, &c.
Bots, you know her?

BOTS
Is there any gentleman here, that knows not a whore, and is he a hair the worse for that?

DUKE
Is she a city-dame, she's so attired?

1st MASTER
No, my good lord, that's only but the veil
To her loose body, I have seen her here
In gayer masking suits, as several sauces
Give one dish several tastes, so change of habits
In whores is a bewitching art: to day
She's all in colours to besot gallants, then
In modest black, to catch the citizen,
And this from their examination's drawn.
Now shall you see a monster both in shape
And nature quite from these, that sheds no tear,
Nor yet is nice, 'tis a plain ramping bear;
Many such whales are cast upon this shore.

DUKE, LODOVICO, &c
Let's see her.

1st MASTER
Then behold a swaggering whore.

[Exeunt 1st and 2nd MASTERS and CONSTABLE.

ORLANDO
Keep your ground, Bots.

BOTS
I do but traverse to spy advantage how to arm myself.

Re-enter 1st and 2nd MASTERS and CONSTABLE; after them a BEADLE beating a basin,[86] then CATHERINA BOUNTINALL, with Mistress HORSELEECH; after them another BEADLE with a blue head guarded[87] with yellow.

[86] *At the carting of bawds and prostitutes they were preceded by a mob beating basins and performing other rough music.*

[87] *Trimmed.*

CATHERINA
Sirrah, when I cry hold your hands, hold, you rogue-catcher, hold:—Bawd, are the French chilblains in your heels, that you can come no faster? Are not you, bawd, a whore's ancient,[88] and must not I follow my colours?

[88] *Ensign.*

Mistress HORSELEECH
O Mistress Catherine, you do me wrong to accuse me here as you do, before the right worshipful. I am known for a motherly, honest woman, and no bawd.

CATHERINA
Marry foh, honest? burnt[89] at fourteen, seven times whipt, five times carted, nine times ducked, searched by some hundred and fifty constables, and yet you are honest? Honest Mistress Horseleech, is this world a world to keep bawds and whores honest? How many times hast thou given gentlemen a quart of wine in a gallon pot? how many twelve-penny fees, nay two shillings fees, nay, when any ambassadors ha' been here, how many half-crown fees hast thou taken? How many carriers hast thou bribed for country wenches? how often have I rinsed your lungs in aqua vitæ, and yet you are honest?

[89] *Branded.*

DUKE
And what were you the whilst?

CATHERINA
Marry hang you, master slave, who made you an examiner?

LODOVICO
Well said! belike this devil spares no man.

CATHERINA
What art thou, prithee? [To BOTS.

BOTS
Nay, what art thou, prithee?

CATHERINA
A whore, art thou a thief?

BOTS
A thief, no, I defy[90] the calling; I am a soldier, have borne arms in the field, been in many a hot skirmish, yet come off sound.

[90] Disdain.

CATHERINA
Sound, with a pox to ye, ye abominable rogue! you a soldier? you in skirmishes? where? amongst pottle pots in a bawdy-house? Look, look here, you Madam Wormeaten, do you not know him?

Mistress HORSELEECH
Lieutenant Bots, where have ye been this many a day?

BOTS
Old bawd, do not discredit me, seem not to know me.

Mistress HORSELEECH
Not to know ye, Master Bots? as long as I have breath,
I cannot forget thy sweet face.

DUKE
Why, do you know him? he says he is a soldier.

CATHERINA
He a soldier? a pander, a dog that will lick up sixpence: do ye hear, you master swines'-snout, how long is't since you held the door for me, and cried to't again, No body comes! ye rogue, you?

LODOVICO, ASTOLFO, &c. Ha, ha, ha! you're smelt out again, Bots.

BOTS
Pox ruin her nose for't! an I be not revenged for this—um, ye bitch!

LODOVICO
D'ye hear ye, madam? why does your ladyship swagger thus?
You're very brave,[91] methinks.

[91] Finely dressed.

CATHERINA

Not at your cost, master cod's-head;
Is any man here blear-eyed to see me brave?

ASTOLFO
Yes, I am,
Because good clothes upon a whore's back
Is like fair painting upon a rotten wall.

CATHERINA
Marry muff master whoremaster, you come upon me with sentences.

BERALDO
By this light, has small sense for't.

LODOVICO
O fie, fie, do not vex her! And yet methinks a creature of more scurvy conditions should not know what a good petticoat were.

CATHERINA
Marry come out, you're so busy about my petticoat, you'll creep up to my placket, an ye could but attain the honour: but an the outsides offend your rogueships, look o'the lining, 'tis silk.

DUKE
Is't silk 'tis lined with, then?

CATHERINA
Silk? Ay, silk, master slave, you would be glad to wipe your nose with the skirt on't. This 'tis to come among a company of cod's-heads[92] that know not how to use a gentlewoman.

[92] Fools.

DUKE
Tell her the duke is here.

1st MASTER
Be modest, Kate, the duke is here.

CATHERINA
If the devil were here, I care not: set forward, ye rogues, and give attendance according to your places! Let bawds and whores be sad, for I'll sing an the devil were a-dying.

[Exit with Mistress HORSELEECH and BEADLES.

DUKE
Why before her does the basin ring?

1st MASTER
It is an emblem of their revelling,

The whips we use let forth their wanton blood,
Making them calm; and more to calm their pride,
Instead of coaches they in carts do ride.
Will your grace see more of this bad ware?

DUKE
No, shut up shop, we'll now break up the fair,
Yet ere we part—you, sir, that take upon ye
The name of soldier, that true name of worth,
Which, action, not vain boasting, best sets forth,
To let you know how far a soldier's name
Stands from your title, and to let you see,
Soldiers must not be wronged where princes be:
This be your sentence.

ALL
Defend yourself, Bots.

DUKE
First, all the private sufferance that the house
Inflicts upon offenders, you, as the basest,
Shall undergo it double, after which
You shall be whipt, sir, round about the city,
Then banished from the land.

BOTS
Beseech, your grace!

DUKE
Away with him, see it done, panders and whores
Are city-plagues which being kept alive,
Nothing that looks like goodness ere can thrive.
Now good Orlando, what say you to your bad son-in-law?

ORLANDO
Marry this, my lord, he is my son-in-law, and in law will I be his father: for if law can pepper him, he shall be so parboiled, that he shall stink no more i' th' nose of the common-wealth.

BELLAFRONT
Be yet more kind and merciful, good father.

ORLANDO
Dost thou beg for him, thou precious man's meat, thou? Hhas he not beaten thee, kicked thee, trod on thee, and dost thou fawn on him like his spaniel? has he not pawned thee to thy petticoat, sold thee to thy smock, made ye leap at a crust, yet wouldst have me save him?

BELLAFRONT
Oh yes, good sir, women shall learn of me,

To love their husbands in greatest misery;
Then show him pity, or you wreck myself.

ORLANDO
Have ye eaten pigeons, that you're so kind-hearted to your mate? Nay, you're a couple of wild bears, I'll have ye both baited at one stake: but as for this knave, the gallows is thy due, and the gallows thou shall have, I'll have justice of the duke, the law shall have thy life—What, dost thou hold him? let go, his hand. If thou dost not forsake him, a father's everlasting blessing fall upon both your heads! Away, go, kiss out of my sight, play thou the whore no more, nor thou the thief again; my house shall be thine, my meat shall be thine, and so shall my wine, but my money shall be mine, and yet when I die, so thou dost not fly high, take all;
Yet, good Matheo, mend.
Thus for joy weeps Orlando, and doth end.

DUKE
Then hear, Matheo: all your woes are stayed
By your good father-in-law: all your ills
Are clear purged from you by his working pills.—
Come, Signor Candido, these green young wits,
We see by circumstance, this plot have laid,
Still to provoke thy patience, which they find
A wall of brass; no armour's like the mind.
Thou hast taught the city patience, now our court
Shall be thy sphere, where from thy good report,
Rumours this truth unto the world shall sing,
A patient man's a pattern for a king.

[Exeunt omnes.

Thomas Dekker – A Short Biography

Thomas Dekker was born around 1572, there is no certainty as to date and it is only probable that he was born in London. Little is known of his early years. From such an unknown start he was however to make quite a name for himself.

By the mid 1590s Dekker had set forth on a career as a playwright. Samples of his work (though not the actual date) can be found in the manuscript of Sir Thomas More. Of more certainty is work as a playwright for the Admiral's Men of Philip Henslowe, in whose records of account he is first mentioned in early 1598.

While there are plays connected with his name performed as early as 1594, it is not clear that he was the original author or part of a team involved in revising and updating. Much of his work has been lost and whilst his prolific output argues against any uniform quality there are undoubted gems both as a solo writer and as part of various collaborations. Indeed between 1598 and 1602, about forty plays for Henslowe, usually in collaboration, can be attributed to him.

Dekker's name first appears in Henslowe's diary* in connection with "fayeton" (presumably, Phaeton) in 1598. There follow, before 1599, payments for work on The Triplicity of Cuckolds, The Mad Man's Morris, and Hannibal and Hermes. He worked on these plays with Robert Wilson, Henry Chettle, and Michael Drayton. With Drayton, he also worked on history plays on the French civil wars, Earl Godwin, and others.

It is also recorded at this time that Dekker's long association with financial mishaps was going to be a life-long concern. He was imprisoned for a short time for debt in Poultry Compter, a small prison run by the Sherriff of London. It was used to house prisoners such as vagrants, debtors and religious dissenters, as well as criminals convicted of misdemeanours including homosexuality, prostitution and drunkenness.

In 1599, he wrote plays on Troilus and Cressida, Agamemnon (with Chettle), and Page of Plymouth. In that year, also, he collaborated with Chettle, Jonson, and Marston on a play about Robert II.

1599 also saw the production of three plays that have survived including his most famous work, The Shoemaker's Holiday, or the Gentle Craft. This play reflects the daily lives of ordinary Londoners, and contains the poem The Merry Month of May. The play reflects the trend for the intermingling of everyday subjects with the fantastical, embodied here by the rise of a craftsman to Mayor and the involvement of an unnamed but idealised king in the concluding banquet. Old Fortunatus and Patient Grissel are the two other surviving plays.

In 1600, he worked on The Seven Wise Masters, Fortune's Tennis, Cupid and Psyche, and Fair Constance of Rome. The next year, in addition to the classic Satiromastix, he worked on a play possibly about Sebastian of Portugal and Blurt, Master Constable, on which he may have collaborated with Thomas Middleton.

To these years also belong the collaborations with Ben Jonson and John Marston, which presumably contributed to the War of the Theatres in 1600 and 1601. To Jonson, Dekker was a hack, a "dresser of plays about town"; Jonson made fun of Dekker as Demetrius Fannius in Poetaster and as Anaides in Cynthia's Revels.

Dekker's riposte, Satiromastix, performed both by the Lord Chamberlain's Men and the child actors of Paul's, casts Jonson as an affected, hypocritical Horace and marks the end of the "poetomachia".

In 1602 he revised two older plays, Pontius Pilate (1597) and the second part of Sir John Oldcastle. He also collaborated on Caesar's Fall, Jephthah, A Medicine for a Curst Wife, Sir Thomas Wyatt (on Wyatt's rebellion), and Christmas Comes But Once a Year.

By 1603, Jonson and Dekker collaborated again, on a pageant for the Royal Entry, delayed from the coronation of James I, for which Dekker also wrote the festival book The Magnificent Entertainment.

At this point Dekker becomes more interested in writing pamphlets; he had done so from the start of his career but now increases his work flow and his playwriting output noticeably declines. It appears also that his association with Henslowe also breaks at this point.

In Dekker's first rush of pamphleteering, in 1603, was The Wonderful Year, a journalistic account of the death of Elizabeth, accession of James I, and the 1603 plague, that combined a wide variety of literary styles to convey the extraordinary events of that year ('wonderful' here meaning astonishing). Its reception prompted two more plague pamphlets, News From Gravesend and The Meeting of Gallants at an Ordinary. The Double PP (1606) is an anti-Catholic tract written in response to the Gunpowder Plot. News From Hell (1606) is an homage to and continuation of Nash's Pierce Penniless. The Seven Deadly Sins of London (1606) continues the plague pamphlet series.

In 1604, he and Middleton wrote The Honest Whore for the Fortune, and Dekker contributed a sequel himself the following year. The Middleton/Dekker collaboration The Family of Love also dates from this time. Dekker and Webster also wrote Westward Ho and Northward Ho for Paul's Boys.

The failures of The Whore of Babylon (1607) and If This Be Not a Good Play, the Devil is in It (1611) left him crestfallen; the latter play was rejected by Prince Henry's Men before failing for Queen Anne's Men at the Red Bull Theatre.

After 1608, Dekker produced his most popular pamphlets: a series of "cony-catching" pamphlets that described the various tricks and deceits of confidence-men and thieves, including Thieves' Cant. These pamphlets, which Dekker often updated and reissued, include The Belman of London (1608, now The Bellman of London), Lanthorne and Candle-light, Villainies Discovered by Candlelight, and English Villainies. They owe their form and many of their incidents to similar pamphlets by Robert Greene.

Other pamphlets are journalistic in form and offer vivid pictures of Jacobean London. The Dead Term (1608) describes Westminster during summer vacation. The Guls Horne-Booke (1609, now The Gull's Hornbook) describes the life of city gallants, with a valuable account of behaviour in the London theatres. Work for Armourers (1609) and The Artillery Garden (1616) (the latter in verse) describe aspects of England's military industries. London Look Back (1630) treats 1625, the year of James's death, while Wars, Wars, Wars (1628) describes European turmoil.

The Roaring Girl, a city comedy that using the real-life figure 'Moll Cutpurse', aka Mary Frith, was another collaboration with Middleton in 1611. The same year, he wrote another tragicomedy; Match Me in London.

In 1612, Dekker's lifelong problem with debt reached a crisis point when he was imprisoned in the King's Bench Prison on a debt of forty pounds to the father of John Webster. He remained there for seven years and continued writing pamphlets during these years but wrote no plays. He did however contribute six prison-based sketches to the sixth edition (1616) of Sir Thomas Overbury's Characters; and he revised Lanthorne and Candlelight to reflect what he had learned in prison.

Dekker also wrote a long poem Dekker His Dreame (1620) cataloguing his despairing confinement;

After his release, he collaborated with Day on Guy of Warwick (1620), The Wonder of a Kingdom (1623), and The Bellman of Paris (1623). He also wrote the tragicomedy The Noble Spanish Soldier (1622) and later reworked material from this play into a comedic form to produce The Welsh Ambassador (1623).

With John Ford, he wrote The Sun's Darling (1624), The Fairy Knight (1624), and The Bristow Merchant (1624).

Another play, The Late Murder of the Son upon the Mother, or Keep the Widow Waking (with Ford, Webster, and William Rowley) dramatized two recent murders in Whitechapel, and resulted in a suit for slander heard in the Star Chamber.

Dekker turned once more to pamphlet-writing, revamping old work and writing a new preface to his most popular tract, The Bellman of London.

Dekker's plays of the 1620s were staged at the large amphitheaters on the north side of London, most commonly at the Red Bull; only two of his later plays were seen at the more exclusive, indoor Cockpit Theatre. The Shoreditch amphitheaters had become identified with the louder, less reputable play-goers, such as apprentices. Dekker's type of play seems to have suited them perfectly. Full of bold action and complementary to the values and beliefs of such audiences, his drama carried much of the thrusting optimism of Elizabethan drama into the Caroline era.

Dekker published no more work after 1632, and he it is thought he died on August 25th, 1632, recorded as "Thomas Dekker, householder". He is buried at St. James's in Clerkenwell.

Most of Dekker's work is lost. His disordered life, and his lack of a firm connection (such as Shakespeare had) with a single company, may have hindered the preservation or publication of manuscripts although perhaps twenty of his plays were published during his lifetime.

*Henslowe's diary
Philip Henslowe was an Elizabethan theatrical entrepreneur and impresario although he had a wide range of other business interests. Henslowe's reputation rests on the survival of his diary, a primary source for information about the theatrical world of Renaissance London.

Henslowe's "diary" is a valuable source on the theatrical history of the period. It is a collection of memoranda and notes that record payments to writers, box office takings, and lists of money lent. Also of interest are records of the purchase of expensive costumes and of stage properties, such as the dragon in Christopher Marlowe's Doctor Faustus, providing an insight into the staging of plays in the Elizabethan theatre.

The diary is written on the reverse of pages of a book of accounts of his brother-in-law Ralf Hogge's ironworks, kept by his brother John Henslowe for the period 1576–1581. Hogge was the Queen's Gunstone maker, and produced both iron cannon and shot for the Royal Armouries at the Tower of London. John Henslowe seems to have acted as his agent, and Philip to have prudently reused his old account book. Hence these entries are also a valuable source for the early iron-making industry.

The diary begins with Henslowe's theatrical activities for 1592. Entries, with varying degrees of detail (authors' names were not included before 1597), until 1609. In the years before his death, Henslowe appears to have run his theatrical interests from a greater distance.

The diary records payments to twenty-seven Elizabethan playwrights. He variously commissioned, bought and produced plays by, or made loans to Ben Jonson, Christopher Marlowe, Thomas Middleton, Robert Greene, Henry Chettle, George Chapman, Thomas Dekker, John Webster, Anthony Munday, Henry Porter, John Day, John Marston and Michael Drayton. The diary reveals the varying partnerships between writers, in an age when many plays were collaborations. It also shows Henslowe to have been a careful man of business, obtaining security in the form of rights to his authors' works, and holding their manuscripts, while tying them to him with loans and advances. If a play was successful, Henslowe would commission a sequel.

Performances of works with titles similar to Shakespearean plays, such as a Hamlet, a Henry VI, Part 1, a Henry V, a The Taming of the Shrew and a Titus Andronicus are mentioned in the diary with no author listed. Most of these plays were recorded when the Admiral's Men and the Lord Chamberlain's Men briefly joined forces when the playhouses were closed owing to the plague (June 1594).

In 1599, Henslowe paid Dekker and Henry Chettle for a play called Troilus and Cressida, which is probably the play currently known as British Museum MS. Add 10449 (the actors' names that appear in the plot connect it to the Admiral's Men and date it between March 1598 and July 1600). There is no mention of William Shakespeare (or for that matter Richard Burbage) in Henslowe's diary (despite the forgeries of John Payne Collier), this is due to the fact that Shakespeare and Burbage were during most of their career not connected to Henslowe's theatre, Shakespeare's company, the Lord Chamberlain's Men, performed at The Theatre (starting in 1594) and later The Globe Theatre (starting in 1599).

Thomas Dekker – A Concise Bibliography

Plays – Sole Authorship
The Shoemaker's Holiday (1599)
Old Fortunatus (1600)
The Noble Spanish Soldier (1602)
Troja-Nova Triumphans, or London Triumphing (1612)
London's Tempe; or, The Feild of Happines (1629)
The Honest Whore, Part II (1630)
Match Me in London (1631)
The Wonder of a Kingdom (1634)

Plays – Co-Written
Satiro-Mastix (1601) with Marston
Blurt, Master Constable (1602) with Middleton
Patient Grissill (1603) with Chettle and Haughton
The Honest Whore, Part I (1604) with Middleton
The Magnificent Entertainment (1604) with Jonson et al.
The Family of Love (1603-1607) with Middleton
Northward Ho (1607) with Webster
Westward Ho (1607) with Webster
The Famous History of Sir Thomas Wyatt (1607) with Webster
The Roaring Girl (1610) with Middleton
The Witch of Edmonton (1621) with Ford, Rowley, &c.
The Virgin-Martyr (1622) with Massinger
The Sun's Darling (1623-4) with Ford
The Bloody Banquet (1639) with Middleton

Non-Dramatic Works
The Wonderful Year (1603)
News from Hell (1606)
The Double PP (1606)
The Seven Deadly Sins of London (1606)
Jests to Make You Merry (1607)
The Bellman of London (1608)
Lanthorne and Candle-light (1608)
The Dead Term (1608)
The Gull's Hornbook (1609)
The Four Birds of Noah's Ark (1609)
The Raven's Almanack (1609)
Work for Armourers (1609)
O Per Se O (1612)
A Strange Horse-Race (1613)
Dekker, His Dreame (1620)
A Rod for Runaways (1625)

Poems
Golden Slumbers Kiss Your Eyes
Beauty Arise
Cast Away Care
The Invitation
Fancies Are But Streams
Here Lies The Blithe Spring

www.ingramcontent.com/pod-product-compliance
Lightning Source LLC
Chambersburg PA
CBHW071309060426
42444CB00034B/1750